VGM Opportunities Series

OPPORTUNITIES IN **DIRECT MARKETING CAREERS**

Anne Basye

Revised Edition

Foreword by
H. Robert Wientzen
President & CEO
Direct Marketing Association

Preface by
Jim Kobs
Chairman
Kobs, Gregory & Passavant

VGM Career Horizons
NTC/Contemporary Publishing Group

Library of Congress Cataloging-in-Publication Data

Basye, Anne.
    Opportunities in direct marketing careers / Anne Basye ; preface by Jim Kobs. —
Rev. ed.
        p.   cm. — (VGM opportunities series)
    Includes bibliographical references.
    ISBN 0-658-00209-0 (cloth) — ISBN 0-658-00210-4 (paper)
        1. Direct marketing—Vocational guidance—United States.   2. Direct
marketing—United States—Case studies.   I. Title.   II. Series.
HF5415.126 .B36   2000
658.8'4—dc21
                                                                                                99-57941
                                                                                                CIP

Cover photograph: © PhotoDisc, Inc.

Published by VGM Career Horizons
A division of NTC/Contemporary Publishing Group, Inc.
4255 West Touhy Avenue, Lincolnwood (Chicago), Illinois 60712-1975 U.S.A.
Copyright © 2000 by NTC/Contemporary Publishing Group, Inc.
Printed in the United States of America
International Standard Book Number: 0-658-00209-0 (cloth)
                                                               0-658-00210-4 (paper)

00   01   02   03   04   05   LB   15   14   13   12   11   10   9   8   7   6   5   4   3   2   1

CONTENTS

How direct and interactive marketing works. The rise, fall, and rise of relationship marketing. How direct marketing started. How Ward's and Sears succeeded. Why consumers and businesses like direct marketing. Why you should consider direct and interactive marketing. One prerequisite: a head for numbers. The future of direct and interactive marketing.

Why direct marketers succeed on the Internet. Opt-in e-mail: a new direct marketing medium. An enormous career opportunity.

Business-to-business direct marketing. The advantages of starting in a direct marketing company. Positions in direct

ABOUT THE AUTHOR

Writer and editor Anne Basye has worked on many direct marketing books, including texts on direct marketing creative strategy, insurance direct marketing, and catalog marketing. Through these projects, she has been fortunate to meet some of the industry's best direct marketing practitioners.

Prior to her writing and editing career, she practiced direct marketing as marketing manager of a line of professional business books sold primarily through direct mail catalogs, card decks, space ads, and packages.

FOREWORD

Question: Why would you—ostensibly a person with his or her eye on the future—consider a career in direct marketing of all things?

Answer: Because you do have your eye on the future. You know a good thing when you see it. And direct marketing today—and tomorrow—*is* a "good thing." Just consider some of the facts:

- *Direct Marketing Is Booming.* In 2000, direct marketers generated an estimated $1.6 trillion, and that's in the United States alone. In 2004, this number is projected to exceed $2.2 trillion.

- *More Jobs Than Professionals.* More than 14.6 million U.S. jobs will be related to direct response sales and advertising in 2000, and that will surpass 17 million in 2004. That's great! Only one hitch: There are not enough well-trained professionals for all these jobs; in other words, there are numerous employment opportunities for you.

- *Not Just Catalog Companies Anymore!* Indeed, virtually every major U.S. industry employs direct marketing. So why do direct response advertising expenditures today represent more than half of total ad spending in the United States? In two words: It works! Direct marketing is targetable, measurable, affordable, and can be used creatively to develop lifetime, one-to-one relationships with customers.

- *Direct Marketers Are E-Commerce Leaders.* Really, this makes sense. After all, what is more "direct," immediate, and interactive than the web? In fact, direct marketers were among the first e-entrepreneurs to actually make a buck in cyberspace—some $18 billion in 2000 and $85 billion projected for 2004. The reason for this early success, simply, is because "traditional" direct marketers hold the expertise that is at the foundation of profitable e-commerce. In other words, they are old hands at order-taking, fulfillment, and customer-focused service and trust building.
- *Direct Marketing Is a Global Business.* If you are interested in international business and policy, direct marketing is for you. Today, thanks largely to the web, direct marketing is truly a business without borders. U.S. companies are marketing overseas. Foreign companies are marketing elsewhere. And direct marketing is going gangbusters in some areas of the world that traditionally had no presence, such as Brazil, Russia, China, India, and South Africa, among other countries.

If any of this sounds of interest, then you're holding the right book. Anne Basye, in a well-written, thoughtful approach, explains this multifaceted industry, outlines the many career opportunities, and describes how some industry leaders got where they are and how they stay there.

Regardless of the professional path you take, I hope you find the joy and passion that I have experienced in my career. Best of luck!

H. Robert Wientzen
President & CEO
Direct Marketing Association
New York City
www.the-dma.org

PREFACE

"A lucky accident." That's how most direct marketers of my generation would describe their entry into the field. But something about this specialized marketing discipline appealed to them, so they stuck with it.

Today it's no longer an accidental career choice for most young people. But it still offers plenty of opportunities to start and build a career. There are three things that I think make direct marketing a special field to work in:

- *Consumers help you make decisions.* Everything in direct marketing is testable and measurable. So you're not making important marketing decisions in a vacuum. Consumers tell you what's working best by the coupons they send in and the 800 numbers they call.
- *Knowledge-sharing.* There has always been a unique openness about most direct marketers. They share their successes and failures at industry conferences and in trade publications. So it's easier to learn what strategies and tactics are successful and apply them to your own job.
- *Growth-driven opportunities.* Even though the direct marketing field is maturing, it's still growing much faster than general advertising and sales promotion. That growth means there are always new jobs opening up and people being promoted. In other words, more opportunities to get ahead and boost your income.

Finally, there's a book to help you evaluate the many career choices in the direct marketing field! Anne Basye has carefully laid out your options and provided concrete examples of how others have launched successful careers in direct marketing. I hope you decide not just to follow in their footsteps, but to make a significant contribution to direct marketing's continued growth in the twenty-first century.

Jim Kobs
Chairman
Kobs, Gregory & Passavant

ACKNOWLEDGMENTS

For their contributions to this book, the author would like to thank the companies and the people interviewed in these pages, as well as the behind-the-scenes people who made those interviews possible. Special thanks go to Jim Kobs of Kobs, Gregory and Passavant; Laurie Spar of the Direct Marketing Educational Foundation; Jack Schmid of J. Schmid and Associates; Phil Walkenshaw and Jonathan Sackett of Townsend Agency; and Karl Dentino of Rosenfield/Dentino, Inc. Many thanks to Nancy Wright Nelson of Wright Nelson & Associates, Inc., for her assistance in providing salary information.

INTRODUCTION

Direct marketing is big business, and it's getting bigger.

Direct marketing has long been recognized as a powerful technique for generating direct orders and sales leads and building retail store traffic. Today it is emerging as the engine driving the e-commerce explosion. Businesses and entrepreneurs are discovering that the principles of direct marketing are the principles it takes to succeed on the Internet. It's no surprise that direct marketing is penetrating companies of all sizes, from the biggest Fortune 100 companies to the newest "dot-coms."

That's because Internet marketing *is* direct marketing. Companies need people who know how to sell without an intermediary. And they need people who understand how to use technology to accomplish marketing goals. That's why an understanding of interactive technology and a solid grasp of direct marketing skills are an unbeatable recipe for success in the job market.

Opportunities in Direct Marketing Careers introduces the wealth of opportunities available in this exciting field. It describes the settings in which direct and interactive marketing is practiced and introduces you to some of the industry's most influential members. You'll discover jobs for people who write copy, people who think visually, people who crunch numbers, and, most of all, people who can couple solid marketing strategy and cutting-edge digital and database technology to turn a web site into a thriving on-line business.

Seven chapters of *Opportunities in Direct Marketing Careers* discuss specific corners of the direct marketing industry: direct marketing and the Internet, direct marketing companies, catalog companies, direct marketing and interactive agencies, telemarketing, the list industry, and database marketing. In these chapters, you'll find out about the qualities it takes to succeed, the range of responsibilities the jobs entail, and the salaries you are likely to earn. You'll also encounter professionals who are pursuing a career in these areas. Among others, you'll meet:

- an agency principle who once ran *Mother Jones* magazine
- a telesales professional who got his start selling tickets to the Policeman's Ball
- a trombone player who founded one of the West Coast's leading direct marketing agencies.

In Chapter 10 you'll find out how to prepare for a career in direct and interactive marketing. In Chapter 11 a panel of distinguished professionals will tell you just how *you* can enter direct marketing.

Direct and interactive marketing is a technique, a marketing channel, and a profession. If you're interested in joining it, turn the page.

CHAPTER 1

DIRECT MARKETING: ITS PAST, PRESENT, AND FUTURE

There's marketing...and then there's direct marketing.

Like marketing, direct marketing involves analyzing the needs of a target audience and considering how best to design, package, and market a product or service that meets those needs.

It means estimating the size of a market, thinking about the competitive environment, pinpointing customer preferences, establishing a customer profile, and devising a strategy to promote the product or service to that customer. But in direct marketing, the customer communication process is far different—and so, often, is the way products actually reach the purchaser.

In the traditional advertising, marketing, and sales process, a product is shipped to a distribution point such as a retail store. Advertising and promotion draw interested customers to the store, where salespeople can close the sale.

Direct marketing uses media to deliver a message that often asks the consumer to purchase through a separate, nonstore distribution channel by placing a direct order through a catalog or an Internet web site. The message also may be designed to generate a request for further information (called a sales lead) or a visit to a store or other place of business in order to purchase a specific product or service (called traffic generation). Billions of dollars are spent on all three messages. In 1998 the Direct Marketing

Association reported that $761.8 billion were spent to generate sales leads, $421.9 billion to solicit direct orders, and $187.8 billion to build store traffic. While consumers were approached primarily by direct mail—with 35.3 percent of orders taking place via direct mail and 27.6 percent taking place on the phone (in business-to-business direct marketing, telephone marketing accounted for 44.5 percent of all sales in 1998)—on-line direct marketing is becoming more common. Spending on interactive marketing and sales exploded in the 1990s from a mere $11 million in 1994 to more than 1 billion in 1999, and it is expected to grow more than 60 percent annually in the early part of the new century.

In his book *Profitable Direct Marketing,* Jim Kobs, Chairman and CEO of the direct marketing agency Kobs, Gregory & Passavant, defines direct marketing this way:

> Direct marketing gets your ad message direct to the customer or prospect to produce some type of immediate action. It usually involves creating a database of respondents.

HOW DIRECT AND INTERACTIVE MARKETING WORKS

Getting a message "direct" to the customer or prospect means using a medium like direct mail or the telephone that can target a specific group of consumers with certain characteristics, instead of a medium like television, which addresses millions of people at a time. In direct marketing, the message always requests a response—the "immediate action" that it seeks to produce.

Responses can take a number of different forms. A catalog or a direct mail package asks recipients to purchase items by placing a mail or telephone order. A direct mail fund-raising appeal is carefully constructed to persuade recipients to make a generous contribution. But costly goods and services like an expensive security system are sold through "two-step" offers, in which people calling in response to a message are given additional information, sent a printed package of material for review at home, and are then called again—sometimes more than once—in an attempt to close a sale.

Whether the response comes by phone, mail, or Internet, it can be measured. This means that the success of every direct marketing offer is evident as soon as all the responses are in. A lot of responses equals a successful offer, while fewer than you predicted means the offer failed.

According to most experts, the classic formula for direct marketing success is to build a list of satisfied customers and then go back to them for repeat sales. That's why a database captures name and purchase information whenever a customer orders a down jacket or a sofa, sends in a check to a charity, or decides to go ahead with a security system installation.

This "house file" is a direct marketing company's most important asset. It can be used to sell additional goods and services or generate revenue by renting those names to noncompeting direct marketers. Even traditional marketers, such as package goods manufacturers, are discovering that communicating with a customer database can boost in-store sales.

At bottom, direct marketing is sales, pure and simple. Although some marketers are beginning to measure its results in terms of image, it is still radically different from traditional image advertising—those million-dollar shots of a bull running through an empty Wall Street, or a canine party animal living it up with beer drinkers. No, direct marketing is *response* advertising—advertising through the mail, in a magazine, over the radio, or on TV that is geared to making a sale. It succeeds or fails on its response: how many people raise their hands and buy the product.

THE RISE, FALL, AND RISE
OF RELATIONSHIP MARKETING

In the old world, and in the early days of the new one, merchants knew their customers' tastes and habits inside and out.

But when the twentieth century rolled around, a rising emphasis on manufacturing began to change the face of retailing in the United States. Small stores and one-to-one selling were pushed aside by large chains that offered lower-priced goods and made money on volume. National brands like Quaker Oats cereal or Ivory soap, recognized by consumers in every corner of the country, did not need to be personally sold. Brand loyalty was built by national advertising campaigns, cost-effective thanks to network radio and television, and national-circulation magazines.

As the "mass market" grew, personal selling began to disappear. Retailers grew less interested in tracking an individual customer's tastes, and more interested in increasing volume through products that met the needs of the larger population. Accessibility, price, and convenience were emphasized over individual service and preferences—until the last two decades, when consumers began once again to pride themselves on their individuality instead of their commonality.

But even during the peak years of the mass market, one corner of marketing was quietly refining its ability to communicate with consumers personally: direct marketing.

When few merchants were bothering to remember preferences and tastes, direct marketers were busy tracking their customers' buying behavior, noting the size, quantity, color, and price of every item their customers purchased, so they could offer similar merchandise in the future. They also were learning more about what made customers open envelopes and consider offers in the first place...what reassurances helped them decide in favor of a purchase...and what incentives helped them pay promptly.

In essence, this attention to customer preferences is what direct marketing is all about. And that is why direct marketing stands poised to help the marketer of today reach the ultimate target: One individual, whose preferences and buying habits can be tracked and catered to—to the advantage of both the marketer and the consumer.

HOW DIRECT MARKETING STARTED

There are historians who will argue that the roots of direct marketing are actually much older, but in the United States it's Mr. Ward and Mr. Sears who are credited with launching and refining the direct mail phenomenon. Both men, based in Chicago, used their "wish books" to market goods to farmers and small town citizens all across the country.

Aaron Montgomery Ward was a traveling salesperson who discovered that he could offer rural customers quality goods at up to 40 percent off if he purchased large quantities of goods for cash directly from manufacturers, and then sold them for cash directly to rural consumers. In 1872 he issued a single-page sheet listing items for sale and explaining how to order them. The single-page sheet quickly grew to 8 pages, and by 1884, Ward's catalog had 240 pages and listed ten thousand items.

As a railroad station agent, Richard Warren Sears took advantage of special freight rates to sell watches wholesale to other station agents, who marked them up and sold them again. When Sears, Roebuck & Company began in 1893, Sears branched out beyond railroad station agents, eventually serving the same largely rural audience developed by Ward. By 1897 Sears, Roebuck & Company had 318,000 catalogs in circulation; by 1907, 3 million.

When Ward's and Sears began, catalog distribution was problematic. The U.S. Postal System was still rudimentary in the late nineteenth century; while urban customers took home delivery of letters for granted, it wasn't until 1898 that Rural Free Delivery brought catalogs and first-class mail directly to farmers and small town residents.

Fulfillment—that is, how packages from Sears and Ward's actually reached rural patrons—was another challenge. Before 1913, the U.S. Postal Service delivered letters only. Packages were shipped via rail or by private carriers like American Express and Wells, Fargo. To receive a package, one had to go to the nearest railroad freight station.

In 1913 the U.S. Postal Service introduced Parcel Post. Within a year, 300 million packages were shipped—a boon to both companies. In the first year of Parcel Post, Sears received five times the number of orders it had the year before, and the increase at Ward's was almost as dramatic.

HOW WARD'S AND SEARS SUCCEEDED

How did two companies in Chicago convince consumers in Nebraska, Utah, Idaho, and other far-flung states to order merchandise they had never seen from people they had never met?

Mr. Ward used a technique that continues to work successfully today, "third-party endorsement." He played up his affiliation with the Grange, a farmers' organization, to build farmers' confidence about buying from Ward's. Testimonials from satisfied Grangers calmed many fears and established Ward's catalog as a real boon to farmers. Both Sears and Ward's overcame customer hesitation with ironclad guarantees: all goods were sent "subject to examination" and any item found unsatisfactory could be returned to the company, which paid for transportation both ways.

Both Sears and Ward's brought a personal touch to their treatment of customers. All letters were responded to, most by hand. This practice persisted even after the typewriter came into use, because the largely rural clientele were offended by "machine-made" letters.

Third-party endorsements and personalization remain important direct marketing techniques today. So do dozens of other techniques discovered earlier this century by direct marketers, who carefully tracked the results of each mailing and determined the factors that improved them. Over the decades, for example, direct marketers observed that:

- Offering a premium to first-time buyers was an effective way to pull in a new customer. (This was first tested in the 1930s, when the Book of the Month Club became a big success by offering free books to subscribers.)
- Some months were better than others for direct mail campaigns. In certain months, a mailing would pull more response; in others, response would be depressed.
- Certain kinds of magazines and newspapers—and certain sections of them—offered a profitable environment for mail-order ads; others just didn't work at all.
- Adding "involvement devices" like "yes" and "no" stickers, plastic membership cards, parchment certificates, "lift" letters, and hand-printed passages helped keep a prospect's attention and encouraged order placement.

These time-honored tactics have been supplemented by a host of more recent innovations that have made direct marketing even more precise and more effective.

First, the victory of the computer over the typewriter and the index card revolutionized the way customer names and purchasing data are recorded.

Next came the discovery that sophisticated demographic data can be overlaid on a list of names to create ever-smaller market segments.

Finally, the advent of credit cards, telephone, fax and Internet ordering, and private delivery services shortened the order and shipment cycle from the old "four to six weeks" to a handful of days.

As a result, direct marketers have developed an almost scientific ability to:

- identify a likely customer
- construct an offer that will appeal to that customer
- write and design a letter or package that the customer will open, read, and respond to
- sell and deliver merchandise quickly.

WHY CONSUMERS AND BUSINESSES LIKE DIRECT MARKETING

Jokes about "junk mail" have been disappearing as millions acknowledge and appreciate the benefits of nonstore shopping. Placing orders by phone, mail, or Internet has become commonplace; in 1998 consumers and businesses spent a total of $1,371.5 billion on direct marketing sales. Telephone marketing and direct mail sales account for about 66.5 percent of these sales. Businesses spent $272.7 billion ordering by telephone and another $161.9 billion ordering by mail. Consumers spent $267.8 billion on mail-order purchases and $209.5 billion on telephone purchases.

Over the years, consumers have come to trust companies that do business by mail, telephone, and the Internet, replacing earlier suspicions that mail-order organizations were shady and mail-order merchandise inferior. Consumers also have responded with delight to the amazing array of marginal luxuries they can order with ease and receive promptly.

Businesses appreciate direct marketing for its versatility. Time has demonstrated that there is almost nothing direct marketing can't sell, especially on the Internet. Today it can be used to:

- sell products directly to customers
- sell corporate season tickets for professional sports teams
- launch new credit cards and attract new credit-card customers
- sell insurance and other financial services
- generate leads and convert them to sales
- generate traffic for retail stores
- establish consumer demand for products that can be converted to retail

"Traditional" direct marketing sales through catalogs and direct mail packages also run the gamut of possibilities. Companies have discovered that they can use the mail, the Internet, and other direct response media to sell:

- books, videos, cassettes, and compact discs
- clothing
- furniture
- fresh flowers
- English muffins
- steaks and wine
- condominiums and retirement communities
- mobile homes
- expensive business equipment and supplies
- automobiles

Thousands of companies are involved in direct and interactive marketing and incorporate direct mail, telemarketing, and the Internet into their everyday sales and marketing efforts.

WHY YOU SHOULD CONSIDER DIRECT AND INTERACTIVE MARKETING

Direct and interactive marketing is at the vortex of marketing change. It's cutting edge. It's exciting. It's effective. And it's mesmerizing to the people who call themselves direct marketing professionals.

Direct marketing is a technique as well as an industry. The situations where the technique is practiced multiply almost daily. A person who understands how to reach and motivate consumers through direct marketing can be an asset to almost any company.

This means that a career in direct marketing will be full of variety. Over the course of a career, a direct marketing copywriter might help set up a web site for a direct marketer of collectible plates, and then move to developing and executing creative strategies and advertising copy for packages that market luxury consumer goods to holders of premium credit cards. Later, he or she might move to the agency side and become a copy supervisor, coaching junior staff through an ever-changing collection of assignments. Eventually, the writer might go freelance or move up to creative director or even head an agency. Opportunities for marketing planners and strategists are just as exciting and just as diverse.

In fact, each place where direct and interactive marketing is practiced is bound to be different. In an agency, you may handle a number of different direct marketing assignments for a number of clients, or just one big one. In a direct marketing company, you will specialize in just one or two lines, developing a deep appreciation for your company's market.

In a catalog company, you may participate in the general management of a catalog or focus on marketing, creating, or stocking certain divisions within it.

You might find yourself managing one or more house lists for a direct marketer or a professional list management company. You might become a list broker, knowledgeable in matching marketers with lists of likely prospects. You might become a consumer data expert who helps marketers design and build proprietary databases and link them to a web site.

You might write copy, design visuals, or manage a product line. You might conduct brainstorming sessions where new creative concepts are generated, or present those concepts to clients. Whatever you do in direct marketing, it will be stimulating and challenging and, in all likelihood, well compensated.

There's one more reason why direct marketing is an excellent choice: it's a career of the future. As the sun sets on mass marketing and rises on micromarketing, direct marketers are ideally positioned to create the brave new world of one-on-one marketing communications that will characterize consumer and business-to-business marketing in the twenty-first century.

ONE PREREQUISITE: A HEAD FOR NUMBERS

Some of the prerequisites for success in direct marketing—ambition, intelligence, stamina, and passion—are necessary to success, in general. Others are more specific to direct marketing. Among these, the biggest one of all is a head for numbers.

Numbers, numbers, numbers. Direct marketing may be creative, but it's also a numbers business. For decades, direct marketers have tracked every variable of every mailing to see just how much each ad or mailing earned, and they have fiddled with packages, products, offers, and media to try and improve response and profitability. In fact, it was direct marketing's accountability that catapulted it to prominence. Just a few of the key mathematical concepts a direct marketer needs to know include:

- *media cost* or *cost per thousand*, obtained by dividing the number of dollars spent on media by the number of direct marketing pieces mailed
- *response rate*, generally calculated as the total number of orders or inquiries received divided by the total number of pieces mailed
- *cost per response*, which is the total promotion budget divided by the total number of orders or inquiries received

- *customer lifetime value,* or how much a customer is worth to you, which determines how much you can spend to acquire him or her
- *recency/frequency/monetary,* which is another formula for determining a customer's potential

A head for numbers also is necessary for testing lists and offers and determining an effort's profitability. In the world of databases, a passing familiarity with statistics is an absolute requirement for those not working directly with programming; for analysts, a solid grasp of advanced statistical and modeling principles and techniques is a must.

Even those involved in the creative side of marketing need an analytical orientation in order to succeed in direct marketing. "The best copywriters and art directors have some of the keenest business minds around," noted Patrice Lyon, a former senior vice president for network development at Ogilvy & Mather Direct.

Fortunately, direct marketing math is taught in college courses and professional seminars. Large employers with formal in-house training programs include it in their curricula. And most direct marketing books devote a chapter or two to describing the basics and how to apply them.

THE FUTURE OF DIRECT
AND INTERACTIVE MARKETING

Direct marketing dominated the 1990s and will continue to be a powerful marketing tool in the twenty-first century.

Between 1993 and 1997 direct marketing sales revenue outpaced total U.S. sales revenue, and growth in direct marketing employment grew more than twice as fast as overall U.S. employment. According to the Direct Marketing Association's 1998 *Eco-*

nomic Impact: U.S. Direct Marketing Today, more than 24.6 million workers were employed in the U.S. economy in 1998 as a result of direct marketing activities—14.0 million in consumer direct marketing and 10.6 million in business-to-business. Of these, nearly 13 million jobs were found in industries that use direct marketing to stimulate demand for products and services; about 427,000 people were employed by catalog companies and related vendors. Another 1.1 million were in advertising agencies, telemarketing firms, and other support services that develop and implement direct response advertising programs. The balance were in suppliers to the direct response industry including printers, catalog fulfillment houses, and credit and collections services.

In 1998 California had the most direct marketing jobs, with 2.830 million employees, followed by New York (1.662 million), Texas (1.645 million), Florida (1.364 million) and Illinois (1.191 million). But opportunities exist in other parts of the country as well.

Nebraska. Omaha is telemarketing central and the toll-free capital of America, home to dozens of catalog companies, credit card servicing centers, and hotel reservation services, not to mention Omaha Steaks, which sells more than $20 million in choice steaks, prime ribs, tenderloin tips, and other seafood and gourmet items to consumers and commercial accounts throughout the United States and abroad.

New England. Home to major insurance companies with direct marketing divisions, plus the grandfather of direct mail, L.L. Bean of Freeport, Maine. Also home to one of the nation's oldest mail-order houses, Orvis, which manufactures and sells $40 million in men's and women's casual clothing, as well as hunting and fishing equipment.

Mid Atlantic states. Day Timers, in Pennsylvania, markets time-management supplies to businesspeople. They manufacture, print, and sell by mail to professionals using a catalog and periodic solo mailings.

Northwest states. Jackson & Perkins, which sells bulbs, ornamental plants, bushes, trees, and award-winning roses by mail to consumers, greenhouse owners, retail nurseries, and garden centers is located here. Their revenues are more than $61 million annually. You'll also find direct mail purveyors of salmon and fruit. Eddie Bauer, too, is located in this region.

For the most part, direct marketing agencies thrive in cities like New York, Chicago, Toronto, Los Angeles, San Francisco, and Boston. But there are hundreds of smaller agencies—and direct marketing experts are needed at thousands of general advertising agencies across the United States and Canada. In short, wherever there are marketing opportunities, there are direct marketing opportunities.

There's no question. The golden days of direct mail and direct marketing are not behind us. A new golden age is here. Especially in our virtual economy, wherever there are marketing opportunities, there are direct marketing opportunities. With more than 29.2 million people expected to be employed in direct and interactive marketing and related industries by 2002, there's a job for you out there.

CHAPTER 2

DIRECT MARKETING
AND THE INTERNET

Williams-Sonoma's on-line store www.williams-sonoma.com and its wedding and gift registry site (www.wswedding.com) draw hundreds of thousands of browsers and buyers. Nike's web store (www.nike.com) is thronged with customers examining everything from soccer shoes to Nike branded apparel. And who doesn't know the story of how Amazon.com shot from start-up to category killer almost overnight?

Stories like these, reminiscent of legends of direct mail businesses launched from kitchen tables, are capturing the imagination of companies everywhere. The Internet is the kitchen table all over again, but this time it's financed by a Wall Street eager to share in the profits of "dot-coms" that transact business on the web.

To these businesses, the Internet offers a level playing field that gives start-ups like Amazon and corporate giants like Nike equal chances for success. But the most successful players have a weapon stronger than great graphics and a cool on-line image: they have strong credentials in direct marketing. Companies like Dell Computers and Williams-Sonoma cut their teeth selling products direct to customers. They know that e-commerce is about closing sales with customers *without* a salesperson—the very heart of direct marketing.

WHY DIRECT MARKETERS
SUCCEED ON THE INTERNET

Direct marketers possess a fount of strategic and tactical knowledge that fits the capabilities of the Internet like a glove.

Direct Marketers Know How to Convert Browsers into Buyers

The millions roaming the Internet won't be converted to buyers overnight. The same click of a mouse that brings prospects to your site can take them to another one if they have no interest in your content. Only when prospects encounter relevant, targeted offers—better yet, when they receive them by opt-in e-mail marketing messages—will they consider making a purchase. Direct marketers are experts at building relationships with customers. They know how to communicate remotely with customers and how to issue "calls to action" that result in sales.

"The digital platform of the Internet makes each contact with the customer infinitely customizable," says Karl Dentino of Rosenfield/Dentino, Inc. "If each customer is assigned a pin number when they log onto your site, it is technologically possible for you to provide information and make offers customized to the individual. The database always made this possible, but traditional printing technology didn't always make it practical."

So, for example, an airline may give you special fares to your most frequent destinations. A credit card company might offer special discounts at the restaurants you visit most often. Or a hotel will extend special rates on the rooms and the restaurants that you like. Car rental firms and telecommunications and financial services companies that don't sell direct via the Internet can still build their brands by offering interactive sites that provide information to help customers in their daily lives. Both applications depend on convincing customers to register on the web site and grant permission for the company to send e-mail marketing messages. The company can develop database profiles of registered customers and use them to tailor messages to the individual. "The bottom line is that instead of sending out a statement insert with the same offer to potentially millions of customers, you can send a different offer to everyone," says Dentino. And it's virtually free.

Direct Marketers Know How to Deliver

Some Internet-based companies sneer at what they call "brick and mortar" businesses. But even the hippest virtual store must have a tangible inventory that it can deliver promptly and reliably to customers. To succeed on the net, an e-commerce enterprise must be able to market *and* fulfill. These "click and mortar" businesses need to blend digital interactivity with solid inventory, supply chain management, and great customer service. Who already has the fulfillment and operations systems that enable them to sell merchandise at a distance? That's right. Direct marketers. Before Williams-Sonoma ever launched a web site, it had tightly run warehouses, top-notch customer service, and unparalleled delivery.

Direct Marketers Know How to Collect and Use Data without Invading Customer Privacy

In a data-rich environment like the Internet, maintaining customer privacy is critical. People won't divulge personal or credit information if they believe your company will make it public knowledge. Direct marketers have worked to develop industry practices that not only seek to balance the interests of companies and individuals, but also conform to state and federal privacy legislation. Industry-sponsored mail and telephone preference programs allow consumers to stop calls and mailings from specific marketers or all of them. Consumers can even cut unwanted mail and phone calls by registering at a web site (www.unlistMe.com) that also lets them request copies of catalogs that do interest them.

Most direct marketing e-commerce sites let customers opt in or out of receiving future on-line marketing messages, and reputable practitioners of opt-in e-mail campaigns include a "remove me" option in every message, although the opt-out rate is less than 1 percent. Business publisher and direct marketer The McGraw-Hill Companies builds trust by posting its privacy policy on all eighty company web sites. In plain language, the policy tells prospective customers what information the company is collecting, how it will use this information, and how it will safeguard the information from tampering, theft, or misuse. Customers can review information collected from them to correct errors and can choose not to have the company share that information.

At the other end of the spectrum are companies that are collecting e-mail addresses and appending them to consumer address and telephone records with the customer's knowledge or approval—a practice experts fear will have negative repercussions.

Opt-in, personalized, targeted e-mail can help e-commerce web sites drive qualified prospects to the site and create ongoing, profitable relationships with its customers. But widespread scamming and unethical data collection may turn off millions of potential consumers who can leave the net the same way they entered—with the click of a mouse! How company data and individual privacy are balanced will determine the future of e-commerce. Direct marketers already are addressing the challenge of finding ways to take advantage of the new technology while allowing consumers to remain in control and retain their privacy.

OPT-IN E-MAIL: A NEW
DIRECT MARKETING MEDIUM

Imagine checking your e-mail and finding a message from an outdoor equipment catalog you patronize. Opening it, you are asked to open an attached file on a new product. Click through to the file, and you're treated to a full-color, animated message about the product, complete with high-fidelity audio.

Sound unlikely? Although full animation and sound are still a dream, text-based direct response e-mail is already a reality. According to Forrester Research, 3 billion pieces of opt-in commercial, e-mail messages were sent in 1997; 250 billion such messages are expected to be delivered annually by 2002. Some of these messages make an offer; others use the e-mail message as the "envelope" and teaser copy that entices readers to click through to a "letter" on a web page or in an attached file. Still others use a newsletter format that includes several short sections, each one a different product or service, each one linked to a web page that provides more information. Text-only messages are quickly giving way to html-enhanced messages that use color, different type fonts and sizes, and visuals. It's already possible to send an e-mail that looks more like a web or catalog page than a memo or letter.

Just like a regular direct mail letter, direct response e-mail messages make an offer and back it up with features, benefits, proof, and other information that buyers need to make a purchase decision. To stimulate response, a free gift is often included. Although the offer is made only to e-mail customers, people can respond via e-mail or by calling.

But there's a big difference between a direct mail letter and an opt-in e-mail message. Direct mail letters are sent to everyone on a particular list. Opt-in e-mail messages are sent only to recipients who have given explicit permission for the company to communicate with them. It's no wonder Seth Godin of Yahoo! has dubbed this kind of opt-in e-mail "permission marketing."

Permission marketing is the child of the marriage of direct marketing science and e-mail marketing. It's changing the way companies communicate and customers respond. The conversion rates are phenomenal. A conventional direct mail campaign may send out 50,000 pieces and get 1,000 responses—a 2 percent conversion rate. Some opt-in e-mail messages can garner "click-throughs" of 10 to 20 percent. But a "click through" isn't a purchase; it's the first step in a two-step process. The first click may take customers to a web page that presents more information and encourages response. In a sense, tracking these clicks is like measuring the number of envelopes opened—something conventional direct mail has never been able to do! Customers who click again, or who call a separate 800 number set up for Internet buyer responses, make purchases. When these sales are tallied, the impact of the e-mail campaign can be quantified.

E-mail offers the kind of interactive relationship with customers and prospects that can only be dreamed about in the postal world. As Karl Dentino says, "The database makes it all possible, but the Internet makes it practical!"

There really is no alternative to permission marketing on the net. A company that tries to send messages to people with whom it has no prior relationship risks being "flamed" by angry people—some of them sophisticated enough to reply with a virus that can shut down an e-mail system. More important, the company is running afoul of existing laws and industry guidelines set up to protect consumer privacy.

AN ENORMOUS CAREER OPPORTUNITY

On-line direct marketing sales are growing quickly as major players begin to do business on the Internet. Sales are expected to top $50 billion in 2003 and ultimately may reach $3.2 trillion. One consultant believes that as much as 10 percent of the U.S. economy will be attributable to the Internet in a few short years, and growth rates are expected to remain in the 50 to 60 percent range.

More than 300,000 people will find work with companies that use direct marketing principles to conduct e-commerce.

Even if, as some pundits predict, a shake out is triggered by the glut of stand-alone e-commerce sites that can't command the profit margins they need to survive over the long run, the job market will remain strong for people with a solid grasp of technology and basic direct marketing principles. For in the year 2000, there are simply too few of these hybrid experts to meet the insatiable demand of companies trying to apply the new interactive technologies to their businesses.

Opportunities abound in the fast-growing interactive divisions of general advertising and direct marketing agencies as well as in independent interactive marketing agencies. USWeb/CKS, the largest interactive shop in 1999, added five hundred Internet-related jobs in just one quarter. These independent Internet professional services companies (also called e-business services) work to fuse marketing strategy and high-level creative with technology. They offer a range of services that encompass everything from designing web banner ads to developing web sites and software. Companies with database capability can connect a company's Internet presence to its computer systems and business processes, link on-line and off-line product inventory, and analyze web site traffic data.

E-mail marketing companies are growing like wildfire, offering opportunities to creatives and marketing strategists who can use this new medium well. Every web-based company needs direct marketing know-how; every direct marketer also needs people who are familiar with technology. Dell.com, Amazon.com, Nike.com—all are hiring people with strong direct marketing skills. A good grasp of interactive technology is icing on the cake.

There's even a demand in related fields such as nonprofit marketing. "We've been advertising a position called an Internet Strategist, and we can't find one," says LMichael Green, Director of

Marketing for CARE, the international aid and development organization. "We are doing some interesting things with our web site, but they meet our needs today. We want a visionary who can assist us in using the power of the Internet to strengthen our mission in the long run—someone who can anticipate our needs five years from now and make sure we are building the right kind of capability and moving in the right direction."

Green isn't finding his Internet visionary among the resumes that hit his desk. "I get resumes from programmers who know all about html, java script, and cold fusion, but nothing about marketing; and from marketing people with no technological knowledge base. I want someone with a direct marketing background who is familiar with the Internet and what it can do. I'm discovering that that's a unique breed."

Jonathan Sackett, Director of Interactive Services for Chicago's Townsend Agency, has experienced the same frustration. "I've found myself dealing with technical people with no relational skills, or people with strong relational skills and no technical grounding. People could give me an idea but not execute it, or execute a program but not come up with ideas."

Career success is a certainty for anyone who can bridge the technology-marketing gap. "People really need to be thinking about developing a bundle of skills," says LMichael Green. Adds Laurie Spar of the Direct Marketing Educational Foundation, "Even people who are studying e-commerce and the Internet need to understand targeted marketing and the customer relationship."

Armed with this background, you jump back and forth between "dot-com" on-line businesses and more traditional direct marketing businesses or agencies. On-line or off-line, one thing is certain: The Internet will influence your career no matter which path you choose to take in direct marketing.

CHAPTER 3

DIRECT MARKETING COMPANIES

At the Bradford Exchange in Niles, Illinois, employees enjoy lunch and coffee breaks at tables nestled among bubbling brooks that wend their way through towering palm trees and a warren of brightly lit, open-plan offices. The sound of running water reaches every corner of the building, providing a soft white noise that helps Bradford employees concentrate on the task at hand: selling limited-edition plates to collectors around the world.

In 1973 Bradford founder J. Roderick MacArthur began importing plates from France, selling them to collectors and dealers. As the popularity of collector's plates grew, he decided to organize the market by developing a medium for buying and selling the most actively traded issues.

Today Bradford operates the world's largest trading center for limited-edition collector's plates, where brokers handle transactions between buyers and sellers. A leader in the direct marketing of collector's plates, Bradford has developed and marketed hundreds of series, from plates illustrated with scenes from *Gone with the Wind* to others featuring work by artists from China, Russia, and Egypt. Other divisions of the company sell collectible dolls, music boxes, Christmas ornaments, and ceramic villages.

The Bradford Exchange is a good example of a company that sells its products primarily through direct marketing media. While it generates sales through space advertising and direct mail, other companies also market through television, radio, package inserts, or any number of media. Unlike catalogs that offer a spectrum of merchandise, these promotions focus on one or two products at a time. For example:

- Omaha Steaks offers choice gourmet meats, seafoods, and hors d'oeuvres to consumers and businesses.
- Wolferman's English Muffins airlifts a dozen varieties of baked goods to breakfast enthusiasts.
- Photo-processing companies offer off-price photo-finishing services with competitive turnaround.

BUSINESS-TO-BUSINESS DIRECT MARKETING

In the business-to-business market, companies sell products and services to businesses through the people who buy for those businesses. Because of the steep rise in the cost of personal sales calls, direct marketing is becoming a more popular way to market products and services to businesses. Today, direct and interactive marketing is used to sell computer supplies and accessories, electronics, office supplies, educational material, books, newsletters, magazines, checks, and specialty business forms.

Some business-to-business companies sell only through direct marketing; others have established a direct marketing arm that supplements their traditional business. Hewlett Packard and IBM, for example, both have divisions that sell their equipment to businesses via Internet and mail-order.

Many of the techniques used to reach businesspeople resemble those used to sell to consumers at home. "A person doesn't change that much when he or she takes off a jogging outfit, puts on a business suit, and heads to the office," notes Jim Kobs. "The main difference is that business buyers are spending company money, not their own. And in the case of many small businesses where the owner is the decision-maker, they are also spending their own money in an office setting."

Businesses also use direct marketing programs to generate leads. A telecommunications company like MCI uses direct marketing telemarketing to solicit new business subscribers. A small business may seek new clients, like the advertising agency that sent a boxed shoe to twenty-five new prospects a week, with a package headlined "Now that we've gotten a shoe in the door." But most business-to-business sales take place through catalogs, which will be examined in Chapter 4.

THE ADVANTAGES OF STARTING IN A DIRECT MARKETING COMPANY

According to widespread industry sentiment, the best place to launch a career is in a direct marketing company or a direct marketing division.

Working on the "client side" can give you a complete education in running a direct marketing program. You can learn everything from targeting an audience and developing a marketing strategy to constructing an offer, creating and producing a package, and maximizing the value of your customers in the "back end."

Knowledge of these phases of the direct marketing cycle is an asset no matter what corner of the industry you end up in. Claude Hopkins, inventor of many of today's direct marketing techniques, began by writing copy for the Bissell Carpet Sweeper Company, where his first sales letter inspired one thousand orders, the first the company had ever made by mail order. Before he founded the direct marketing agency Stone & Adler, Bob Stone sold surgical bandages by mail to first-aid departments of manufacturing companies and later oversaw all direct mail for a business publishing firm. These aren't isolated examples. A whole host of direct marketing luminaries began on the client side.

POSITIONS IN DIRECT MARKETING COMPANIES

Marketing

Direct marketing companies offer challenging positions in marketing and advertising. Entry-level *marketing assistants* handle administrative and reporting work for product managers but also are given some responsibility for marketing lower-volume lines.

Assistant product managers assume complete responsibility for marketing medium-volume lines to current and new customers. This entails planning, developing, executing, and analyzing new direct response campaigns, expanding the customer base, and projecting and monitoring sales volume and expenses.

Product managers and *senior product managers* have complete marketing responsibility for one or more top-selling lines, as well as supervisory and management responsibility for their subordinates. Generally, the higher up the product management ladder one goes, the more involved a person gets in companywide strategy and management issues.

Managing a product line entails the following:

- deciding price points
- constructing offers and guarantees
- determining mailing schedules and markets
- tracking and analyzing sales trends
- looking at response and making any necessary modifications to marketing plans and programs
- working with media people to choose media vehicles that will attract new prospects
- trying to discover more information about the market, its characteristics, and its potential, using the research department's skills
- working with creative staff to come up with a marketing strategy that can be executed creatively and effectively
- working with letter-shop people to make sure that deadlines are met and mailings go out on schedule
- calculating profit and loss on mailings

A product manager makes sure that promotions are going out, product is being shipped, customers are paying, and revenue goals are being achieved smoothly and flawlessly. *New customer acqui-*

sition professionals expand the customer base by devising promotional campaigns that will bring new clients to the house file and by researching and purchasing outside media such as magazines, Sunday newspaper magazines, television, package inserts, catalogs, and some outside lists.

Most direct marketing companies have an in-house *list manager* who manages the house file—the database that contains buying histories and demographic profiles of all current customers. The list manager maintains the database, enhances it with additional demographic data as needed, and promotes it to list brokers and other direct marketing companies that wish to offer a noncompeting product or service.

Creative

Writers, artists, and *designers* build the creative campaigns that are used to solicit customers. They work hand-in-hand with the marketing staff, who present the creative staff with a profile of a market, information about the product, and a marketing platform or strategy from which to generate ideas for the creative presentation.

Proofreaders and *editors* check all copy before it is laid out and proof it again before it goes to the printer. Sometimes proofreaders and editors who are interested in becoming copywriters are given small writing projects to try their hand at. Those who display a real gift for copy can move up, along with *copywriter trainees,* who are challenged to write copy for products as soon as they are hired, albeit for less-profitable lines.

Copywriters are charged with creating effective, product-specific copy that persuades prospective customers to make a purchase. Early in their careers, copywriters may focus on smaller projects, while *senior copywriters* handle projects for important, high-volume products or services. But regardless of their position on the career ladder, copywriters must choose the right voice for each product and craft convincing, persuasive copy that effectively covers the marketing and creative platform devised by the marketing team.

"To realize that one of your ideas, something you wrote and helped to create, may have made a very profitable difference in response, or even just convinced one more person to buy a plate—that's very satisfying for a writer," notes a former copywriter for the Bradford Exchange. "You know that people all over the world are reading your work—and liking it."

Writing copy means knowing everything about the product you're promoting and the people you're promoting it to. "No salesperson would dare knock on doors without first learning all about the product. How it works. How it's made. How it differs from competing products," creative expert Martin Gross once reminded copywriters. At a company where copywriters are assigned specific lines, immersing oneself in its products and customers is both a possibility and a requirement. (In direct marketing agencies, where copywriters bounce from project to project, becoming well versed in a product can be harder.)

Art directors are charged with making a package or ad succeed visually, by taking a concept and copy and:

- illustrating it
- choosing a clear type face and designing type blocks
- choosing headline faces
- providing input on paper stock and ink colors
- coordinating the "look" of every component in a direct mail package, from the brochure and the letter to the order form, outer envelope, and buck slip (a separate slip attached to a piece)

For direct marketing beginners, the road into art direction begins in graphic design. *Keyliners, typesetters,* and other graphic design staff prepare the final art for the printer. Facility with desktop publishing and illustration programs is an absolute requirement in this area.

Traffic coordinators schedule the production of jobs and handle the administrative duties that, neglected, can derail a project: staying on top of paperwork, making sure writers and art directors meet their deadlines, and routing copy, art, and mechanicals for approval. In some companies, traffic coordinator is an entry-level job with a future, but in others, it's not even a rung on the career ladder.

The Interactive Team

Many companies are assembling interactive teams charged with finding new ways to use the Internet to relate and sell to customers. In one major technology company, the interactive team's strategic objective is to know, value, and target its customers. To meet that objective, the team is developing relationship marketing programs by collecting customer names on the web, "mining the data" to identify prospects for new purchases and upgrades, and developing on-line communications to customers.

To build the database, team members are creating incentives to encourage customers to register on the company's web site. On the registration form, the customer can indicate whether he or she wants to receive future communications from this company and is also assigned a user identification password. These passwords—very common in e-commerce—store a customer's profile and preferences so that when the customer visits the site, he or she is directed right to the screen or area desired. Credit card data also are stored to make purchasing faster. The password enables the company to track who visits the site and how often.

Two kinds of incentives—intrinsic and extrinsic—are offered to encourage customers to register. Intrinsic incentives are benefits that naturally come with registration. Customers who register will get better and faster support, more news about product updates, and have a better experience working with the company. Extrinsic incentives are akin to traditional direct response offers: a 50 percent discount on their next purchase from a "dot-com" site or a free magazine subscription. "Our intent is to make registration easy and compelling," says one team member.

Customer names gathered through registration go into a company's database. Previously the company's database served as a giant electronic address book, primarily used to contact customers for product recalls. Now the team is building a database that will drive marketing by enabling the company to personalize e-mail message content to specific customer segments or even individual customers.

The team's *customer knowledge manager* uses the classic direct marketing formula of RFM (*r*ecency, *f*requency, and *m*onetary value of customer purchases) to sift through the database and find customers for specific offers. (In some companies, the customer knowledge manager also collects the data and manages the database.) She or he "mines the data" by applying statistical analysis to the vast company database to find buyers who are likely to buy a second printer or respond to a cross-selling effort. When customer valuation and segmentation techniques have identified high-spending customers with a very high "lifetime value," the company will develop a customer loyalty program designed to reward the most valuable customers. By giving these customers a significant reward, like access to priority queuing for technical support, the company hopes not only to retain their business but to encourage others to spend more in order to join the group.

The *electronic messaging manager* uses this customer information to create content for e-mail marketing messages that deliver news and offers to registered customers who have "opted in" or agreed to receive them. News grams blend news items with promotions for new products and link each feature through a hot link to the company's web site, where readers can learn more about a product or access a vendor. In the near future, the team anticipates sending html e-mail messages that include miniature web pages in the message.

The team's goal is to create retention or "stickiness"—to get customers to access the company's site often and to stay a while before jumping to another site—as well as to drive purchases at its e-commerce site.

MARKETING COLLECTIBLE PLATES: BRIAN COVEY

Plates from the Bradford Exchange aren't what you use to set the table.

Some are shaped like cookie jars cut in half. Some are three dimensional and include sculpted animals. Some are battery operated and light up or play music. One plate includes an angel's wing with real feathers.

"We push the envelope on the definition of a plate," says Brian Covey, Assistant Product Manager, who manages twenty lines of three-dimensional plates that feature sculpted, cast, and hand-painted figurines like animals, flowers, and Disney and Warner Brothers characters.

Brian, who holds an M.B.A. in marketing from the University of Wisconsin, is part of a cross-functional team that works together to develop and market plates profitably. To introduce a new plate, team members from product development, marketing, and advertising meet to review the concept and discuss advertising approaches. Often new concepts and prices are tested to better gauge what appeals to Bradford customers. "We use statistical analysis," says Brian. "We don't make these decisions until the results are in."

Test results are used to segment Bradford's enormous customer list to find likely buyers for the new plate. "Using statistical data from test responders, we can build a probability model and predict purchasing behavior based on how customers fit within the model," Brian explains. While Bradford's database experts actually build the models, it's up to Brian to interpret the statistics and find profitable segments to mail.

Deciding to whom and when to mail is one of Brian's biggest responsibilities. He monitors Bradford's house file for new names to mail. "Our list changes constantly," he says. "If a new two-dimensional Disney plate does well, I'll mail an offer for one of my three-dimensional Disney plates to everyone who purchased. I spend a significant amount of time performing analysis on particular segments to mail. I then have to review my decisions with my manager."

Brian also looks outside the Bradford house list for new customers, especially for products that don't exactly match the taste of the typical Bradford customer, a middle-aged woman with traditional or conservative values. Space advertising in *TV Guide* and Sunday newspapers brought in buyers for a Mark McGuire plate.

Brian works with advertising to develop mailing packages and makes sure that the right components—brochures, letters, envelopes, etc.—are delivered in the right quantities. He also monitors inventory and decides whether sales of a plate warrant additional production. After a year or two, he may decide to close a line. "We produce limited editions, so we don't offer the same product year after year," Brian explains. "Our customers are always looking for something new and fresh."

Although the Bradford Exchange its known for its analytical approach to direct marketing, Brian's job isn't all analytical. His creative judgment comes into play during product development, when he may recommend a change in color palette, and in advertising, when he might suggest adding die-cut brochures, special inserts, or an elaborate certificate to a mailing package. Even the many reports he generates offer a creative outlet. "We gather large amounts of data through creative marketing," he explains. "Sometimes there's so much it can be a challenge to present it in a clear, concise manner to my superiors." On the whole, Brian estimates his job is 70 percent analytical and 30 percent creative. "Basically, my job is to make good decisions for my line."

SALARY RANGES

Although salary levels may vary from company to company, salary ranges are fairly consistent. Keep in mind that the benefit packages a company offers—such as educational reimbursement programs and profit sharing—can add a great deal to a person's take-home pay.

The following salary figures and the salary figures quoted in chapters 4, 5, 7, and 8 were provided by Wright-Nelson Enterprises, Inc., an executive search firm specializing in recruiting for the direct marketing industry.

Product management

Product management trainee	$32,000–35,000
Assistant product manager	$35,000–45,000
Product manager	$45,000–65,000
Senior product manager	$65,000–90,000

Marketing

Entry-level marketing trainee	$30,000–40,000
Assistant marketing manager	$35,000–50,000
Marketing manager	$50,000–75,000
Senior marketing manager	$75,000+

Creative

Entry-level creative assistant	$25,000–35,000
Copywriter or art director	$32,000–55,000
Associate creative director	$50,000–80,000
Creative director	$80,000+

CHAPTER 4

CATALOG COMPANIES

Consumer and business catalogs exploded in the 1980s, built on their strengths in the 1990s, and are holding their own in the new century, although many shoppers are migrating to the Internet. In 1998 slightly more than 425,000 people were employed by the catalog industry, which mails billions of catalogs annually to homes and businesses. In recent years the ranks of catalogers have swelled as retailers launched catalogs to make direct sales, build store traffic, and promote their web sites. Businesses, too, have found catalogs a convenient way to expand cost effectively; using a catalog a distributor can easily expand from a single state to ten, or a company can "disintermediate," that is, get rid of distributors altogether by selling direct to customers.

Of all types of direct mail pieces sent to consumers at home and people at the office, catalogs are the most accepted. Their popularity stems from a long list of benefits that consumers respond to.

Convenience. Catalogs let consumers shop whenever they want, making them especially useful for all sorts of working people. Jim Kobs of Kobs, Gregory & Passavant calls them "stores that never close."

Product variety. Catalogs bring an appealing and diverse array of products into the home for consideration. And since catalogs are distributed to carefully targeted groups of people, chances are good that the catalogs a consumer receives closely reflect his or her taste, interests, and purchasing power.

Complete product information. In many cases, the product photo and accompanying description tells more about a product's features, benefits, and applications than the average store clerk could convey.

Reliable guarantees. As catalog retailing has grown, so has consumer confidence in the quality of catalog-sold products and the exchange and refund policies that back them up.

Prompt shipment. Most catalog items are on their way to customers within twenty-four hours of receipt of order, and they are delivered in three or four days. During the Christmas season, major catalog companies guarantee that orders placed by December 23rd will be delivered by the 25th. Large business catalogers like Quill promise that orders received by noon will be delivered the next day; same-day delivery may soon be the standard for business catalogers.

Off-site warehousing. Quick and reliable delivery of commodities like office or cleaning supplies means that business customers can order just as much as they need—and let the catalog company foot the bill for warehousing and inventorying the materials.

The old "wish books" of Sears Roebuck and Montgomery Ward would look like dinosaurs in today's catalog market, which is dominated by specialty catalogs aimed at precise segments of consumer interests. In Canada, Sears still publishes more than six thousand catalog pages in "big books" and niche publications; in the United States, J. C. Penney also continues to mail a big book. But on a fall afternoon, a typical mailbox may be overflowing with these catalogs:

- Williams-Sonoma: upscale kitchenware and accessories
- Lands' End: high-quality casual apparel for work and play
- Vermont Country Store: reasonably priced "old fashioned" clothing, linens, and home tools and accessories with a "country" flavor

- Wireless: CDs, cassettes, books, T-shirts, and gift items for public radio listeners
- Smith & Hawken: gardening tools and accessories
- The Sharper Image: cutting-edge home electronics, computers, and other high-tech goods

Business catalogers also are highly niched, although each one does its best to offer a full line of products within that niche. Quill, profiled later in this chapter, supplements its full-line office products catalog with dozens of specialty catalogs that offer complementary merchandise to highly targeted segments. Lab Safety Supply sells industrial safety equipment; the highly regarded New Pig Corporation catalog includes materials for cleaning up oil in machine shops and chemical, biological, and other spills; and Galls, recently named Catalog of the Year by *Catalog Age* magazine, carries a full line of equipment for police and firefighters.

Each of these catalogs is a shopper's dream and a major employer. Catalog employment is expected to continue to grow, with business-to-business catalogers experiencing somewhat healthier growth. People seeking jobs in the industry will find that the line between consumer and business-to-business catalog companies is porous; professionals find it easy to make the transition from consumer to business catalog and vice versa.

CATALOGS AND THE INTERNET

Today's catalog customers are migrating to the Internet as consumer, retail, and business catalogs set up on-line stores. The Internet's convenience is unrivaled: Credit card orders are secure, and these on-line stores-without-walls can be accessed twenty-four hours a day by anyone anywhere in the world with a web address—even people who aren't on the catalog's house list. In fact, in 1999, 65 percent of customers ordering via Internet were *new* to the catalog they were ordering from—good news for a business that depends on new customers to grow.

While some catalogs have set up separate e-commerce divisions, others have chosen to integrate e-commerce throughout the company. "We view e-commerce activities as an integral part of our business," says Leslie Weber, Vice President and Chief Information Officer of the Quill Corporation. Marketing, creative, and management information systems (MIS) all need to be involved in operating an e-catalog. Although the paper catalog is secure in the near term, many catalogers look forward to the day when most new and existing customers turn to the web to order, and the millions of paper catalogs now mailed are whittled down to a more cost-efficient number.

THE CATALOG PRODUCTION CYCLE

A catalog company's work flow follows a process illustrated in Figure 4.1, created by catalog consultant Jack Schmid. Figure 4.2 shows the time frame for when these steps occur. Merchandising, marketing, and creative all work together over an eighteen-month period to fine-tune each issue of a catalog, measure its results, and then apply what it has learned about products, audience, and creative to subsequent issues. Let's look at the responsibilities of each area.

Merchandising

Merchandising plans, develops, sources, and purchases the items included in the catalog. Because most catalogs are merchandise driven, merchandising personnel play a leading role in creating and stocking the "store" every season and inventing new concepts for start-up catalogs.

Generally speaking, merchandising consists of two major areas—merchandising planning and inventory control. Merchandising planning is responsible for creating and planning catalogs that will be published in the coming year; inventory control monitors current demand and orders items as needed for circulating catalogs.

Figure 4.1 The Catalog Process

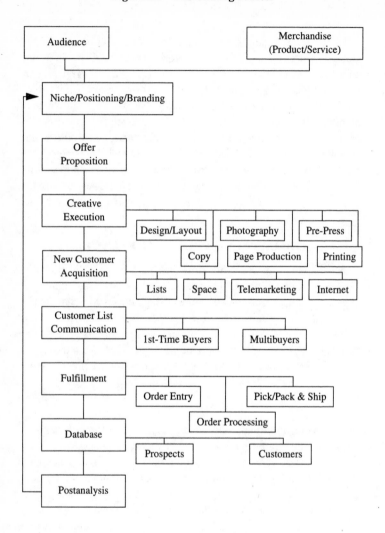

Figure 4.2   Typical Eighteen-Month Catalog Planning and Production Cycle

July 2001
Begin planning for fall '02 catalogs.

August 2001
Develop plans for individual catalogs.

September 2001
Planning committee reviews plans.

October 2001
Merchandising reviews plans.

November 2001
Purchase imports for fall '02.

December 2001
Planning committee reviews plans again.

January 2002
Buyers at market.

February 2002
Buyers at market.

Lines are closed—i.e., merchandise is selected.
Buyers begin negotiating terms with vendors.

March 2002
Buyers continue negotiating terms on selected merchandise.

March–April 2002
All product information turned over to creative staff.

May–June 2002
Fall copy and art created and reviewed.

June 2002
Merchandise begins arriving.
Warehouse screens and enters into inventory.

Circulation plan drawn up and mail dates booked.

July 2002
Fall '02 catalogs begin to mail.

August 2002
Inventory control monitors sales reports to forecast demand.

August–October 2002
Inventory monitored: reorders placed, P.O.s adjusted or canceled as needed.

October–December 2002
Inventory problems managed.
Inventory control reacts to back orders and cancels.
Overstock is liquidated.

Merchandising planners have the happy task of searching out new items for a catalog. In some instances, that may mean developing a product—in an apparel catalog, for example, finding a pattern, choosing a fabric, deciding where to manufacture the product, and selecting a vendor. Also called *buyers,* they are creatively and financially responsible for a line of merchandise. They select and develop product and have plenty of input into how their line is displayed in the catalog. Less experienced *assistant* or *associate buyers* help select and plan merchandise, pull together product information for the creative team, and work with creatives as they develop pages. Buyers generally have retail experience or have worked in product management.

In very large operations, buyers and assistant buyers may be overseen by merchandise managers who draw up and execute an overall plan for a division, handle vendor issues, project sales volume, and plan product mix.

Inventory management staff analyze current demand in order to project future demand and determine whether a given item should be repeated in a future catalog. They are responsible for making sure that "SKUs" or stock-keeping units are in stock in just the right quantity—enough to prevent back orders, but not so much that overstock is created. In a very large catalog operation, inventory management specialists may be responsible for one or two departments; in an apparel catalog, that may be men's suits or women's blouses. On the management control side, catalog companies look for people with some experience in retail management, purchasing, or finance and strong analytical and computer skills.

Marketing

Marketing professionals influence the creative cycle, too. Marketers oversee plans for expanding a catalog's sales and build and manage the customer base by analyzing response, calculating the profitability of items and pages in the catalog, examining customer profitability, and planning strategies to increase average orders and response rates.

The marketer's cycle of analysis and planning helps keep future catalogs on target. For example, when marketing identifies profitable best-sellers, those items can be given more space in a future catalog so that they can sell even more. A successful quarter-page item might grow to half a page, and if the results are really spectacular, it might win a high-profile full page or be placed on a "hot spot" like the back cover.

Marketing, then, crunches the numbers that refine, reinforce, or alter merchandising's "hunches." Its basic responsibility is to figure out how best to market the catalog to new and existing customers. Some marketing staff focus on developing new and "spin-off" catalogs. When a new catalog is proposed, these professionals help decide what its focus and purpose will be. They define the new catalog's target audience and conduct competitive analyses of potentially competitive catalogs. This customer-definition process also occurs every time a new edition of an existing catalog is planned.

Circulation staff devise plans for catalog distribution. They determine which customers in the master or "house" file will get which books, when, and how often. To attract new customers, they may create special catalog editions to send to prospective customers, choosing mailing lists and developing circulation plans for the new editions. They also may develop space ads or seek alternative media that prompt prospects to request a catalog or purchase an item.

A catalog's house file of customer names is managed by *database personnel,* who analyze customer purchase history to determine the offers and prices most likely to retain current customers and add new ones. *Market research specialists* design surveys and conduct focus groups to learn more about customers, sometimes with the help of a market research firm.

Creative

In the creative process, creative directors, writers, and artists work closely with merchandising and marketing staff to give the catalog an image that will appeal to its market. This is where copy is written, products are photographed, typefaces are selected, and pages are designed and laid out. Production personnel who purchase graphic arts services like color separations, paper, printing, and binding are also part of this process, which is outlined in depth in Figure 4.3.

The creative process begins with a conceptual kick-off meeting. Attended by merchandising, marketing, and creative staff, the meeting begins by reviewing the performance of the previous catalog and its merchandise. Competing catalogs are examined; the niche, positioning, and brand of the catalog is reviewed; and new merchandise is presented before attention turns to the creative appearance of the forthcoming catalog. When the meeting adjourns, all staff leave with a schedule and lists of "to do" assignments.

Phase two of the creative process focuses on layout, photography, and copy. *Art directors* and *senior art directors* must be thoroughly familiar with a catalog's niche, brand, merchandise, and market so that they can design a catalog that will catch the customer's eye. They must know exactly why a particular item was selected, what its major benefits are, and how it can be presented in an appealing layout. Art directors provide detailed sketches of each product shot to photographers, who light and design photos.

Copywriters get product specifications and rough layouts from the creative team and write copy to size that entices customers and conveys product information, often in a very small block. As creative expert Tom Collins once pointed out, "Writing for a catalog is a rather minor art form, somewhat akin to writing a Japanese haiku." Copy must be brief, but concise; it should deliver all the important selling points in a persuasive way. Another creative expert, Don Kanter, says, "In catalog copy, there is nobody to answer questions. The writer must anticipate literally every question that could arise in the mind of the prospect and answer that question in the copy." In large organizations, a copywriter may move up to *senior copywriter* and *copy director.* Copy directors oversee and review copy and work with art directors and merchandising staff to

Figure 4.3 The Catalog Creative Process

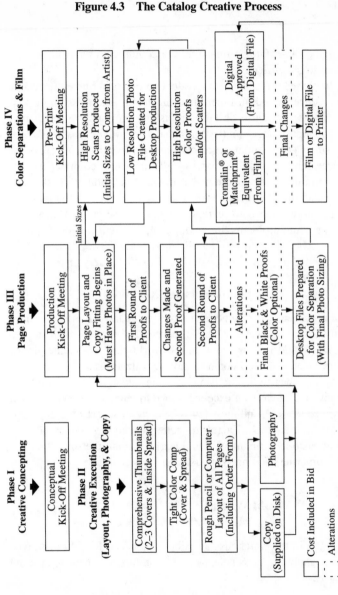

develop the catalog's image and direction, communicating these ideas to the writers.

In phases three and four, production personnel take the designers' concepts and turn them into finished pages. *Desktop* or *page production staff* use desktop publishing programs to select type and compose pages on the computer. The *graphic arts production manager* gets estimates, selects vendors, negotiates prices, determines schedules, and supervises all film work, color separations and printing, and paper to make sure the final catalog's look meets expectations. Production staff work vigilantly to ensure that printing is in register, color is representative of the product, deadlines are met, and problems that might compromise a catalog's appearance, schedule, and profitability are avoided. They also see to it that rented mailing lists are delivered to the bindery on time.

Fulfillment and Operations

Fulfillment, also called operations, is the last but often the most critical step in a catalog's selling cycle. Because all the lush photography and inviting copy in the world can't overcome sloppy fulfillment, most top-notch catalog organizations assign considerable firepower to this division. In some catalog organizations, this "back end" area is an excellent place to launch a career. In other organizations, spending a few weeks here is part of every newcomer's orientation. There's no better way to see sales trends and meet customers firsthand, while learning about the snags that can hold up orders and prevent customer satisfaction.

FROM WAREHOUSE TO DIRECTOR: ROSS LONGENDYKE

A job in the warehouse at Talbot's launched Ross Longendyke on a cataloging career that, to put it mildly, has had its ups and downs.

After graduating from the University of Michigan in 1984 with a degree in economics, Ross moved to Boston, where he joined Talbot's as Assistant Operations Supervisor. In that capacity he supervised hourly employees who packed and shipped 130,000 units of women's clothing every week to Talbot's 110 retail stores. After a stint as Operations Supervisor, he was promoted to Merchandise Distributor and allocated apparel to 120 stores and planned assortments for future stores. His years at Talbot's introduced him to the basics of retailing and cataloging and sharpened his inventory management skills.

In 1989 he moved to Chicago, where he spent the next four years attending the school of hard knocks. Three jobs at three major companies were ended by downsizing, landing Ross in the unemployment line three winters in a row. "I still get nervous every December," he laughs.

The first job was at Spiegel, where he served as Assistant Buyer, Inventory Control, for the consumer electronics division. "ABICs," Spiegel's entry-level merchandising personnel, track sales projections and daily back-order reports to find out how much of each item is available and whether sales are on target. If sales of an item were running under or over projection, Ross consulted with vendors and coordinated the best way to service the demand or liquidate excess inventory. If a shipment was delayed while demand was strong, he arranged air shipments to avoid a back-order situation.

Soon he was promoted to Business Planning Coordinator, where he provided forecasting and back-end analyses to people throughout the company. To track competitors, he searched information on-line, kept a library of press clippings, and amassed copies of competing catalogs. Because Spiegel's recent profits had come from its specialty catalogs, Ross analyzed the performance, circulation, and marketing strategies of defunct specialty Spiegel catalogs to see whether any should be revived, and then he studied competitors for new ideas for spin-offs. "I knew a lot about high-level decisions within direct marketing, but I had never done a merge-purge and didn't even know how to cut a postage check," he remembers. "In a way, I was putting the cart before the horse." The position was eliminated when Spiegel suffered a downturn and reorganized its marketing department.

Ross was quickly hired by GRI Corporation as an Assistant Marketing Manager for the World of Beauty Continuity Club. For the first time, he had hands-on responsibility for creating telemarketing and space ad programs to attract new buyers and for forecasting sales volumes for fulfillment based on response, attrition, and returns curves. But GRI was on its last legs, and the company closed nine months later.

His next stop was Sears Roebuck. Desperate to salvage its catalog division, the giant retailer was supplementing its big book with specialty catalogs. For the light-truck book and the big-and-tall clothing book, Ross analyzed merchandise performance, often using "squinch," or "square inch analysis," to determine the sales-per-inch of catalog space for each catalog product. Based on the results, he would recommend that a product be allocated more or less catalog space. But the end was near for the catalog division, and when Sears shut it down, Ross faced his third and last jobless January.

A recruiter brought him to Wolferman's Muffins in Kansas City, Missouri. In almost seven years at Wolferman's, Ross has added depth to his experience and vaulted from Assistant Manager to Director of Direct Marketing. "Now I have soup to nuts responsibility for all of Wolferman's catalogs," he notes. "I'm responsible for developing catalogs and mailing pieces; developing and executing merchandising, marketing, and circulation plans; prospecting for new customers and segmenting our house list; and analyzing the results of each catalog." Although Ross also manages Wolferman's two-million-name customer list, he does not oversee customer service or fulfillment.

Like many food and gift catalogs, Wolferman's business is seasonal; 80 percent of its annual sales are rung up in November and December. Ross spends spring and summer creating and printing the fall book, developing circulation plans, and renting lists. When his five Christmas mailings are finished, he joins customer service in handling the nitty-gritty of taking orders and facilitating returns—an opportunity that teaches him plenty about the wants, needs, and priorities of Wolferman's customers. Orders peak steeply the first two weeks of December, and then the mad scramble is on to deliver 500,000 boxes in time for Christmas.

Ross has no plans to leave Wolferman's, but he hopes someday to serve as general manager of a catalog. "My years at Wolferman's have done wonderful things to crystallize what I have learned," he says. "It brought together all of my piecemeal experience and taught me a great deal about cataloging. I've seen cataloging in the big-company context and the small-company context, and I know my future is in small-company cataloging."

THE QUILL CORPORATION:
A BUSINESS-TO-BUSINESS CATALOG GIANT

The Quill Corporation is the nation's leading direct marketer of business products, and it distributes more than eighty million business products catalogs annually to businesses worldwide. Quill, with annual sales of over $700 million, is headquartered in Lincolnshire, Illinois, has ten distribution centers located throughout the United States and Europe, and employs more than twelve hundred people.

One hundred percent of Quill's business is conducted through direct marketing, but it wasn't always that way. When Jack Miller founded the company in 1956, he relied on personal sales calls— until he discovered the power of the penny postcard. After a few mail campaigns proved to be vastly more profitable than pounding the pavement, Mr. Miller concentrated entirely on selling through direct mail.

According to Kyle Anderson, Quill's Vice President of Marketing, the main difference between consumer and business-to-business catalogs lies in order frequency and size. Because Quill's customers order at least twice a month and place fairly large orders, the company works hard to build long-term customer relationships. "We mail customers our full-line catalog and then contact them frequently with mailers that offer new products and special offers. It's a little like grocery shopping," he says. "A sale may draw people in for some specially priced items, but then they pick up bread and milk. Our short-term offers prompt people to place an order, but first they check the full-line catalog for staples."

Another difference between Quill and most consumer catalogers lies in their approach to marketing. "Many consumer catalogers focus on products and then find people to buy them," Anderson explains. "We start with customer segments like schools, professional services, health care, and government and try to bundle our products and services to address their needs. For each customer group, we develop different versions of the catalog, different pricing structures, and different contact strategies." Each time a customer buys, Quill captures information about the transaction in its powerful database, which it uses to plan future customer contacts.

Much of the transactional information comes from Quill's web site, www.quillcorp.com. "There's a nice synergy between the Internet and our paper catalogs," Anderson points out. "Buying office supplies is something a typical person doesn't like doing. Through e-commerce, we can make ordering easier. Using our on-line catalogs, customers can find additional information about our products. They can find out when an item is in stock and how long it will be before an out-of-stock product is delivered." Quill is actively seeking new ways to combine paper catalogs and the Internet to build sales and provide better customer service.

Because e-commerce is so important, Quill looks for people who are proficient in computers and understand interactive and digital media. Quill stores all copy and photos digitally and transmits pages from the computer to the printer without using paper or film. While digital media let Quill produce dozens of specialty catalogs very quickly and cost effectively, they also have changed many job descriptions. "Once, a writer just wrote copy and handed it to someone else who laid out a page by hand, who gave it to someone else to turn into film," says Anderson. "Now we want writers who can use Quark. When their copy is approved, they use templates provided by art directors and drag in a photo here, put copy there, and assemble the page on screen." Computer proficiency is a must in these positions.

Quill's entry-level marketing position, the Market Assistant, assists market managers in analyzing mailings and mailing lists and preparing product information for the creative staff to use to prepare pages. "Our business is very analytical," says Anderson. "We need people who know statistics and are comfortable working with the database. Creative remains an important element in the catalog business, but data drive the business today."

Because Quill's web site is managed by another company, its employees don't need to have cold fusion and html programming skills. Not yet, anyway. "Anyone going into cataloging has to be ready to explore this new opportunity," says Leslie Weber, Vice President and Chief Information Officer of Quill. "E-commerce will become the primary way of doing business with the next generation, and we have to prepare for it now. Once, everybody ordered by mail; now everybody orders over the phone using a paper catalog; over the next ten years, people will order on-line with an on-line catalog."

Kyle Anderson agrees. "Electronic commerce will be a big part of the catalog business in the future, and it is essential to understand it." When the on-line catalog becomes commonplace, Quill will be ready.

SALARY RANGES

Salary ranges for various jobs in catalog merchandising, marketing, and creative are given below.

Merchandising

Assistant buyer	$35,000–45,000
Buyer or inventory control specialist	$35,000–60,000
Merchandise manager	$60,000+

Marketing

Entry-level assistant	$32,000–40,000
Mid-level planner	$40,000–55,000
Manager	$55,000–85,000
Vice president/marketing	$85,000+

Creative

Entry-level assistant	$28,000–40,000
Copywriter or art director	$35,000–65,000
Associate creative director	$65,000–85,000
Creative director	$85,000+

Fulfillment

Vice president, fulfillment	$100,000+

CHAPTER 5

DIRECT MARKETING AGENCIES

Nearly every major advertising agency has acquired or formed a direct response or interactive division. General agencies that do not have subsidiaries are "integrating" direct marketing by hiring specialists to assist on general accounts. In addition, there are hundreds of independent agencies that specialize in direct and interactive marketing; a growing number tackle interactive alone. The top agencies and their billings are listed in Appendix B.

On the whole, direct marketing agencies are organized like general advertising agencies. There are account executives, creatives, and media people—but their functions and emphases are somewhat different. In general agencies, big clients spend money on image and awareness in an attempt to create a rosy long-term sales trend. But direct marketing campaigns are structured to elicit an immediate response—an order, a purchase, a sale, or an inquiry—and follow up on that response with a new offer, thereby building a relationship between customer and direct marketer. This focus on measurable response and an ongoing relationship influences the thrust of every procedure, from designing and writing space ads and direct mail packages to purchasing media.

Some direct response agencies will handle a client's direct marketing business only, taking a pass on general advertising assignments. The largest agencies and networks try to keep client work in the family, dividing assignments between their general agencies and their direct response subsidiaries. Smaller agencies may specialize in a certain segment of direct marketing, such as business-to-business direct marketing, catalog marketing, broadcast direct marketing, or fund-raising.

In this chapter, we'll look at the job opportunities in direct response agencies, and then take a close look at two quite distinct agencies: Townsend Agency and Leo Burnett NorthStar.

ACCOUNT MANAGEMENT OPPORTUNITIES

Account services or account management personnel take primary responsibility for the relationship between the agency and its clients. Success in this area requires a unique blend of talents:

- a keen grasp of marketing strategy and a sincere interest in helping a client's business grow
- a solid grounding in digital media
- a willingness to live, breathe, and understand a client's business, inside and out
- an ability to sensitively prevent or resolve misunderstandings between the client and members of the agency team
- strong negotiation and presentation skills, often developed through sales experience
- a gift for tracking and tending to details
- solid quantitative skills that can be used to "work the numbers," and a facility for understanding the significance of results

These talents are called on daily, as members of account services help develop the client's marketing strategy and coordinate the many agency departments involved in creating and implementing a direct response program.

Job titles within account services sound similar but have distinct responsibilities. At the top of the pile is one or more *vice president of account services* or *director of client services,* who oversees account supervisors and makes sure that all accounts are running smoothly, that the workload is distributed evenly, and that agency profit goals are being met. The vice president of account services also participates in presentations to potential new clients.

Account supervisors have management and strategic responsibility for one or more accounts. They pinpoint client problems, pull together the people and meetings needed to solve them, and keep an eye out for new business opportunities that might develop in existing accounts. They have profit responsibility for their accounts and participate in agency management matters as well as new business presentations.

Account executives play a more tactical role on their accounts. Experts in how to get things done in the agency, account executives make sure creatives, production people, and other departments are contributing their best to their accounts. They participate in or lead proposal presentations to client contacts on their accounts. Other responsibilities include:

- estimating a project's cost and preparing the estimate for client review
- when a client is printing a piece, setting up meetings with client vendors to make sure production goes smoothly
- working with clients to get response figures (not always easy, as clients may not be willing to share response figures, or may only release partial figures)

The entry-level position in account services is associate account executive. At Townsend, profiled later in this chapter, an associate account executive supports the rest of account services by:

- scheduling projects from their conception through the mail or broadcast date
- taking notes on the creative strategy and reviewing it with creative staff
- assisting the agency team in presenting a proposal to the client and occasionally handling the presentation of a single component of the project, such as a buck slip or an insert

- taking notes during all client meetings and preparing and distributing the client conference report, which recapitulates all decisions made in the meeting
- keeping in touch with the client for missing information, creative elements, and so on, and routing all versions of art and copy past the client for approval
- working with the traffic coordinator to make sure the project is on schedule
- making sure mailing lists, magnetic tapes, postage check, and other elements of the mailing process are in order so that the mailing deadline can be met
- preparing client invoices

The associate account executive also may go on press checks and photo shoots, research mailing lists, and prepare sample books for clients.

Aspiring associate account executives should have a bachelor's degree in business administration, communications, or advertising; at least a year of agency experience; and extremely strong organization and communication skills. Digital skills are a must.

TRAFFIC

Entry-level opportunities abound in traffic, which can be a terrific place to learn the agency business.

The traffic coordinator is responsible for coordinating the component parts of a direct marketing project within the agency. Traffic people monitor (and sometimes establish) timetables and deadlines to see that they are met. They make sure that the components of a project with multiple pieces are produced simultaneously, so that all pieces are available when needed. They interface with everyone involved in a project—account service people, creatives, production, and media vendors—and gain an enviable expertise in just exactly how and when the pieces of a project fit together.

People in traffic must be able to manage a myriad of details under tight deadline pressures. But the payoff to this traditional entry-level job is a comprehensive knowledge of the direct marketing production process and an ability to remain cool in high-pressure situations. Both qualities come in handy in account services and production, two areas into which traffic personnel are frequently promoted.

MEDIA

As in a general agency, people in media research plan and buy a client's media. The difference, of course, is that all the media selected are response media: mail-order lists, telemarketing lists, response-prone broadcast segments and print media, and interactive electronic media.

In planning space for a direct response print ad, for example, a media assistant looks for a magazine with a good response record—not a coffee-table book, because people are reluctant to mar a beautiful book by ripping out a coupon. When buying television, the direct response media buyer looks for nonprime-time slots when reruns and other less-engaging shows are programmed, because viewers who are engrossed in a prime-time show or movie don't call or even write down 800 numbers. Matching the right list to the right client or offer is similarly delicate; planners must find consumers with the right demographic characteristics or buying habits who also have indicated a willingness to purchase by mail.

The media department is an excellent place to launch an agency career. Entry-level media personnel—typically called *media assistants*—collaborate with people throughout the agency as they help select and purchase lists, space, and time, and assist in analyzing the results of campaigns. Media assistants coordinate orders with brokers and publications, meeting all pertinent deadlines. They also sharpen their negotiating skills by bargaining for premium positions or time slots at the best rates possible.

In a large agency, media assistants are eventually promoted to *media planner* or *media buyer.* Using syndicated data, rate cards, *Standard Rate and Data's* guides to print media and mailing lists, and other sources, planners research and select all the media that will be used during a campaign. Some planners also purchase media, although broadcast purchases are generally handled by buyers, whose only job is to purchase media. Some planners and buyers specialize in print, while others specialize in broadcast or lists.

Large offices can have as many as forty people working in media. Smaller agencies will have fewer, and responsibility for planning and purchasing media will overlap. Some smaller agencies have no separate media staff. In these agencies, account services personnel handle some of the planning function but delegate media buying to freelancers or an outside media buying service.

Successful media people possess analytical minds, excellent communication skills, and a basic curiosity about new and emerging forms of media.

CREATIVE SERVICES

A direct marketing agency's creative staff falls into two camps: those who work with words, and those who work with pictures.

Copywriters participate in the strategy and planning sessions in which an agency develops its concept for a client's project. After that, they closet themselves with art directors to bring that concept to life.

Copywriters must be able to communicate persuasively and concisely. But a gift for language must be complemented by a keen sense of marketing. In direct response agencies, the *raison d'être* of all copy is to sell. Fancy, clever, self-conscious prose—unless it delivers the selling message *and* increases response—is a no-no. An intimate knowledge of the audience being targeted—what it wants, why it buys, how it reacts—is essential.

Copywriters generally start off as *assistant* or *junior copywriters*. In smaller agencies, they are responsible for proofing copy as well as writing it. *Copywriters* and *senior copywriters* handle more prestigious accounts and play a bigger role in crafting and executing the client's creative strategy in conjunction with the art staff. A *copy supervisor/director* manages copywriters, motivating them, reviewing their work, boosting morale when work is rejected, and monitoring work flow and deadlines. At the very top is *vice president/creative director,* who supervises both copywriters and graphic arts staff.

Art directors and *assistant art directors* transform a project's creative strategy into a tangible design that makes the selling message as relevant and as tantalizing as possible. Weaving color, type, and illustrations around and through a copywriter's words, these artists create visual reasons to buy or inquire. Some of their specific duties include:

- attending strategy meetings
- conceiving a multiplicity of ideas and illustrating them in pencil sketches for account team discussion
- providing the rationale for the creative execution—in other words, explaining why certain colors or graphics were chosen
- preparing and revising comprehensive layouts and working with keyliners on final art boards
- arranging and directing photo shoots
- reviewing final art boards and proofs

PRODUCTION

Most direct mail packages contain a dozen different components, all of which must be conceived of, designed, and produced individually. To the production staff falls the responsibility for turning finished art and copy into a 6" × 9" package with an outer envelope, a letter, brochure, order card, buck slip, lift letter, and reply envelope.

People who succeed in production are detail oriented, able to work under pressure, and thoroughly familiar with production processes and suppliers. Through their efforts, the component parts of a package are printed so that final colors match PMS swatches, final dimensions are precise (so that all the components will fit into the outer envelope), and postal regulations and size standards are accommodated.

Production people also work hard to stay abreast of rapidly changing reproduction technology and postal regulations. They are experts on computer typesetting, design, and reproduction; ink-jet and laser-printing processes; gluing and binding technologies that can affect a print ad with a reply card inserted in a magazine; as well as printing the perforated gummed stickers that fill every mailing from Publishers Clearing House.

Production managers are responsible for estimating, purchasing, and coordinating the graphics arts services required to produce a project. In very large agencies, a production manager might oversee a staff of *production coordinators* or *production buyers,* who each would assume responsibility for certain projects.

Proofreaders and *typographers* work to make sure that copy is free of errors and professionally set. *Keyliners* and *layout artists* (sometimes called "wrists") make sure that the art director's concepts become mechanicals that can be reproduced correctly.

RESEARCH

In the old days, research meant testing—mailing two versions of a package to the same list, and seeing which one drew the higher response. While testing remains a fundamental research function, research techniques formerly associated with general agencies are beginning to penetrate direct marketing.

Very large agencies have research departments whose employees direct consumer surveys, focus groups, and other research vehicles and techniques as client needs dictate. Smaller agencies retain an outside service to handle research assignments, with agency and client input.

Research professionals should have a strong background in research methodology, quantitative and behavioral statistics, and psychology or sociology. An M.B.A. can be helpful.

DATABASE MARKETING

As the power of a strong database is recognized, more agencies are hiring experts who can help clients develop, maintain, and benefit from a database marketing program. These professionals can assist clients in:

- determining the kinds of information needed for targeted marketing
- gathering and enhancing the data
- planning marketing programs that take advantage of the database or turn it into a profit center

Database experts must combine a knowledge of computer sciences, management information systems, and statistical analysis with real marketing savvy. At Townsend, the Director of Database Marketing is responsible for translating the clients' data-related and operational marketing needs into solutions that support immediate and long-term initiatives. Entry-level titles are *analyst/programmer, program coordinator,* and *technical support manager.* In smaller agencies, account staff may consult on a database's potential, then help a client select an appropriate vendor for database management services rather than handle it themselves.

INTERACTIVE OPPORTUNITIES

Many agencies have opened interactive divisions to position themselves squarely in the middle of today's fastest-growing opportunities. Hundreds more independent agencies focus only on interactive direct marketing.

Also known as Internet professional services or e-business services, these independent agencies work to adapt new and existing enterprises to the Internet economy. Both independent agencies and interactive divisions seek to fuse the disciplines of strategy, creative, and technology together, which until recently was as hard to combine as oil and water.

These shops and divisions offer a wide range of services. Leo Burnett's interactive division, Giant Step, offers web-site and software development, consulting, and interactive ad planning and placement. Townsend develops and hosts web sites with content as well as transaction and interactivity capabilities, and can tie those sites into a client's database. Others partner with back-end technology developers to connect a company's Internet presence to its computer systems and business processes. J. Walter Thompson, for example, outsources back-end support as it would outsource production services for a commercial.

Townsend Agency's interactive team is led by thirty-year-old Jonathan Sackett, who serves as Director of Interactive Services. Other team members include a network engineer who makes sure Townsend's three internal computer networks, which host client web sites, run smoothly. Interactive art directors design programs using graphics and animation, and interactive developers execute the interactive art director's designs.

One of Townsend's interactive team's biggest tasks is to educate clients about the direct marketing capabilities of the Internet. Many companies are still stuck in the "pretty picture" phase of the Internet and need prodding in order to move into e-commerce activities. Others may have plunged in and developed a web site but omitted something essential like the device that enables the search engines to locate a site. Without these significant items, someone surfing the net is unlikely either to stumble on the site or find it intentionally.

The interactive team and Townsend's database staff function as the agency's marketing technology group. Recently the group developed an on-line program designed to boost usage of the GTE Airphone. Townsend's database department put GTE's database on its computers, figured out how to link back GTE customer information to the GTE web site, and designed a program that took advantage of the Internet's ability to personalize a marketing message. When customers logged onto GTE's web site, they typed in a pin number. Townsend's database retrieved information about the customer's cellular phone usage and then made an offer tailored to his or her pattern. "By coupling the Internet and the client's database, we were able to get the right message to the right person at the right time in the right medium," Sackett explains.

TOWNSEND AGENCY

A gleaming office just east of Chicago's O'Hare airport is home to Townsend Agency, an award-winning mid-sized agency whose clients include Discover Card, GTE Airfone, Kemper Funds, NEC Technologies, Reebok, and the American Medical Association.

Founded by Phil Walkenshaw and Gary Tillery in 1979, Townsend grossed just $63,000 in its first year. Walkenshaw (who majored in philosophy and was once general manager of *Mother Earth News*) and Tillery (who majored in Latin American studies and worked in Indonesia and Singapore during the early 1970s) attracted their first clients by promising they would "beat their control"—in other words, by swearing that Townsend could create a direct mail package that would pull more response than a client's existing package. The challenge worked, and twenty years later, the company had billings in excess of $40 million.

Townsend started out marketing hard products but quickly found a niche in marketing intangibles such as financial services, insurance, and clubs. It also has built an enviable track record in new products, successfully launching more than fifty new products and services.

When Gary Tillery retired, the agency's first employee, David Ives, joined Chairman and CEO Phil Walkenshaw as COO. The partners reinvented the agency, placing even greater importance on building and managing customer relationships. Today Townsend seeks to integrate communications so that its clients speak to their customers with one voice, whether they communicate through a catalog, a web site, or a direct mail piece. "What we do is manage our client's relationship with their customers," says Walkenshaw. "Although we have always been—and will always be—built on a platform of sound direct marketing principles, we call what we do now Integrated Relationship Marketing (IRM)™. We help our clients acquire and manage customers by accumulating database information and using that database to find new customers, keep existing ones, and revive dormant customers."

Townsend has fifty employees in account services, creative, database, interactive, traffic and production, general management, and administration. By and large a young agency, the employees work in teams to tackle and solve direct marketing problems.

"A new client's problem will be defined by a group account director, along with the account supervisor who will be handling the account," says Walkenshaw. "Once the problem is defined, we let our creatives loose on it. Then, at what we call a 'heads meeting,' the writer, the art director, the traffic coordinator, the production person, the account person, and a principal all get together to review preliminary executions. The creatives take the feedback into consideration and then work up the creative that will ultimately be presented to the client."

The popularity and potential of the Internet is changing the way Townsend helps its clients communicate with customers and prospects. In the late 1990s it launched an interactive services department led by Director of Interactive Services, Jonathan Sackett.

The interactive team tackles a variety of projects. Its members create web pages for the Internet, Intranet (an Internet system accessed only within a company), and Extranet (Internet service accessible only to approved external parties). They design e-commerce programs that use cutting-edge technology and great Internet design to find ways to make a client's web site make money—a popular service in an era when most web sites lack an e-commerce focus. The team also creates digital and CD Rom presentations and CD cards and is developing programs to meet the huge demand for opt-in e-mail.

"At Townsend, we believe that people are adults," says Phil Walkenshaw. "By and large, they don't need supervision. We set high standards, and the people who work here consistently surpass them." Walkenshaw's claim is backed up by an impressive array of awards garnered by Townsend people, including four Echo Awards, an international Mobius, and several first-place Tempo Awards.

According to Phil Walkenshaw, the best way into an agency career is to come from the client side. That's where he started, when he served as director of marketing for The Bradford Exchange, the collectible plates company profiled in Chapter 3. "Starting on the client side gives you an appreciation of the client-agency relationship from the client's perspective," he notes.

On the account side of the agency, he says, it's best to start as an assistant account executive, or in traffic. "In traffic, you learn how an agency works. That knowledge coupled with a willingness to learn and the right personality can take you far. Two of our former traffic coordinators have gone into account management and have done very well."

In a mid-sized agency like Townsend, an associate account executive must be able to hit the ground running. "Large agencies can give employees a formal training program, but we can't. We offer something more akin to an apprenticeship—we expose our assistant AEs to plenty, and ask them to work hard."

On the creative side, experience counts. Townsend Agency has never hired an art director right out of school. It looks for art directors who come equipped with experience, a fat portfolio, and

MacIntosh experience. Production artists and keyliners occasionally are hired straight out of school. Because Townsend Agency has invested so much in computer graphics software, it rarely goes outside for graphic services.

"Small and mid-sized agencies are easier to get into than large agencies, and they give their employees more responsibility," Walkenshaw points out. "New hires are exposed to more, so they learn more. When someone goes on vacation, somebody else takes over that desk. That means you get to handle a greater breadth of assignments."

LEO BURNETT NORTHSTAR

Founded in 1999, Leo Burnett NorthStar is the direct marketing and promotional arm of Leo Burnett Company, prominent in advertising since its founding in 1935.

NorthStar as a stand-alone unit formalizes Burnett's direct marketing, sales promotion, and interactive approach, capabilities that have existed at the agency since 1986. Previously, the agency pursued an integrated approach, assigning direct marketing specialists to specific departments such as media, research, and client service. "It was a little like assigning the members of the Montreal Canadiennes hockey team to different major league baseball teams and telling them to teach baseball players how to play hockey," says Tim Claffey, NorthStar's Executive Vice President and Managing Director. "Try as you might, hockey just isn't a baseball player's sport."

With Claffey at the helm, the agency's approach has evolved into a resource committed to building an integrated and creative direct database and promotion program for world-renowned brands. A team of 150 direct marketers in Chicago and Toronto works closely with clients, in some cases serving as agency of record. Two prominent clients are Oldsmobile and Walt Disney World.

To launch the Disney Cruise Line, NorthStar developed a direct response television campaign to stimulate new customers to book cruises and designed a strategy for encouraging repeat bookings. For Oldsmobile, NorthStar creates programs to entice targets to test drive Oldsmobile cars. For the Internet portion of its work, NorthStar collaborates with Burnett's interactive division, Giant Step.

Summer internships are one path into NorthStar, and the agency does hire people straight out of college. Positions as copywriters, assistant art directors, and assistant account executives are offered to beginners willing to work hard. Once part of the agency, employees can benefit from NorthStar's generous training budget and tuition reimbursement program. While seminars on digital media like the Internet are most common, about fifteen employees are studying improvisational comedy through Chicago's Second City. "Improv training unlocks a lot of little rooms in everybody, and that shows in their work," Claffey explains. "It brings out the best in people creatively and interpersonally, and it makes them much better presenters."

Prospective NorthStar employees need to be smart, energetic, and computer-savvy, says Claffey. "Digital knowledge is absolutely essential. We also look for people with multidiscipline potential, who are prepared to work in a world of multiple markets, media, and technology."

Good communication skills are also important. "We want people who communicate well, not people who say *sort of, I'm like, yeah,* and *for sure.* Well-rounded people who are smart, understand the technology, are personable, and can communicate are the future stars our agency can mold. Good people like that will move up the career ladder at NorthStar."

SALARY RANGES

Account management

Account coordinator	$28,000–35,000
Assistant or associate account executive	$35,000–45,000
Account executive (higher at large agencies where account executives may supervise very large accounts)	$35,000–55,000
Account supervisor	$55,000–75,000
Management supervisor	$75,000+

Creative staff

Entry-level copywriter	$30,000–40,000
Copywriter or art director	$40,000–65,000
Associate creative director	$65,000–85,000
Creative director	$85,000+

Media

Media coordinator or assistant	$25,000–35,000
Media buyer	$35,000–45,000
Media planner	$40,000–55,000
Media manager	$50,000–75,000
Media director	$75,000+

Traffic and production

Traffic coordinator	$25,000–35,000
Graphic arts assistant/keyliner	$30,000–45,000
Production manager	$50,000+

Interactive services

Director of interactive services	$80,000–100,000
Interactive technology manager	$80,000–120,000
Interactive account executive	$50,000–70,000
Interactive creative director	$60,000–80,000
Interactive graphic designer	$40,000–60,000

CHAPTER 6

TELEMARKETING

As a teenager, Art Sobczak had a flair for telephone sales. He could sell anything—even tickets to the Policeman's Ball. After earning a degree in marketing at Creighton University in Omaha, he was all set to go into business for himself when he was offered a job in 1982 as a telemarketing sales specialist with AT&T Long Lines.

From the Bell Systems Sales Center in Kansas City, Art sold small businesses on the concept of telemarketing. First, he found out as much as he could about what a business did. Then, he helped the business identify how it could benefit from telemarketing. Once the benefits were pinned down, he worked with his prospect—usually an owner or manager—to identify the phone system that would help the business realize those benefits. Finally, he signed them up for AT&T 800 or a WATS-line. All told, each sale took from one to ten phone calls to close. The resulting sale added up to between $50 to $5,000—all sold by phone.

One year later, at age twenty-three, Art's urge to be an entrepreneur had not diminished, so he set up his own company, which specialized in telemarketing consulting and training services. In addition, he became the director of Outbound Telemarketing for a telemarketing service agency in Shawnee Mission, Kansas, where he put together telemarketing programs, hired and trained new telephone marketing representatives, and evaluated and reported on programs to clients. As if running a business and a service agency weren't enough, he also launched a newsletter, *Telephone Selling Report,* which coached telephone sales representatives on what to say and how to say it on the phone.

"After juggling all those balls for a year—running my consulting business, publishing a newsletter, and managing the telemarketing service agency—I found I wanted to focus more on sales than operations. So I joined WATS Marketing as national sales manager for outbound telemarketing, targeting large accounts like regional Bells and consumer products," Art remembers.

Soon thereafter he was asked to join WATS Marketing's sister company, First Data Resources (both were subsidiaries of American Express), where he took a position purchasing direct marketing services. "Eight months of coordinating inserts for credit card statements was enough. I went back to my business and have focused on it full-time ever since."

His business, Business by Phone, focuses on training telephone marketing representatives and helping them boost their sales. As an acknowledged expert in the field, he runs seminars, has developed video and audiotape programs, and continues to publish *Telephone Selling Report,* as well as a catalog of training products. He also has written three books on telesales and published five others.

THE TELEMARKETING REVOLUTION

Art Sobczak lives in a corner of the world where telemarketing has become a major industry. Ideally situated in a central time zone, telemarketers in Nebraska can work from 8:00 A.M. until past 11:00 P.M. to reach consumers in every U.S. time zone. A convenient time zone and a cutting-edge telecommunications system (installed because of the large number of defense installations in Nebraska) have enticed catalog companies, credit card servicing centers, and hotel and airline reservation centers to Omaha, the "toll-free capital of America."

But it isn't only in Omaha that telemarketing is surging. In some industries, telephone sales have practically replaced face-to-face sales calls. In others, telephone marketing campaigns have doubled the effectiveness—the "pull"—of mail campaigns. As telephone equipment gets more sophisticated, and as people feel more and more at ease handling business by phone, telemarketing and telesales are sure to grow even more.

Why is telephone marketing so popular? For one thing, the telephone is a very flexible and personal medium. Unlike direct mail pieces or broadcast advertising, where the message is "frozen" before production, a telephone script can be modified as needed, in an instant. In sales, it offers the intimacy of a person-to-person conversation without the expense of a traditional sales route—car maintenance, gasoline, hotels, "downtime," and so forth.

The telephone also provides immediate results. Whether a telephone campaign or a telephone sales call has been successful is quickly apparent. Reviewing a day's phone calls can reveal:

- how many sales, leads, or orders were generated per hour or day
- how many calls it takes to make a sale
- the variety of reasons an offer is refused, compared to how many refusals were logged
- the geographic distributions of sales and refusals

As versatile as it is effective, telemarketing can accomplish dozens of marketing and sales goals. On its own, or in conjunction with a direct mail campaign, it can be used to:

- test-market new product and service ideas
- promote special time-limited offers to existing or potential customers
- increase the size of customer orders by upgrading an order, for example, by suggesting add-ons or special additional offers and incentives. Add-ons are merchandise added to an order after or as it is being placed. Usually, the customer service

representative who takes the call or a telephone communicator who places a call to a consumer will suggest related merchandise of interest

- handle consumer problems and inquiries promptly, conveniently, and personally
- generate leads for salespeople, or explore leads to make sure they are genuinely "hot" before a salesperson follows them up in person
- raise funds for nonprofit and political organizations
- enhance a database by learning more about customers as they call in or are contacted

The icing on the telemarketing cake is its low cost. Selling, generating leads, or accepting orders by phone can lower the cost of each sale, which is an attractive factor in any industry.

But consumers do not always react favorably to telephone calls. Many state legislatures have enacted legislation that restricts a company's ability to contact people who are not already its clients. Even without state and federal legislation, the popularity of unlisted telephone numbers, answering machines, and caller I.D. make it difficult for telephone communicators to reach consumers at home. That's why, although consumer telemarketing continues to be used to market everything from magazine subscriptions and credit cards to carpet cleaning, the real growth is taking place in business telemarketing.

THE SIZE AND SCOPE OF TELEMARKETING

More than 300,000 firms incorporate telephone marketing as a channel of marketing and distribution. Approximately sixty-two billion dollars were spent on telemarketing in 1998, accounting for 44.5 percent of all business-to-business direct marketing sales.

Business Week magazine estimated that by the year 2000, there would be more than eight million jobs in telemarketing. Some of these were in reactive or inbound telemarketing, where a consumer called the telemarketing center to reserve a ticket for an airline, a sporting event, or an opera, or to order merchandise. The rest were in proactive or outbound telemarketing, in which the telemarketing representative placed calls to customers or prospects.

Inbound and outbound telemarketing are practiced in several settings:

- within agencies devoted to designing and running telemarketing programs for clients, and placing or accepting phone calls
- within major consumer marketers such as Sears, which calls customers to sell add-ons like extended warranties or additional insurance policies
- within catalog companies like Lillian Vernon, which accepts calls from customers ordering merchandise and also calls customers to offer related merchandise, such as a pair of headphones to go with a stereo set
- within major business-to-business companies, whose inside sales staff can profitably cover very large territories or service marginal accounts by phone

How telemarketing is applied—and how telemarketing personnel are compensated—vary considerably.

Telemarketing Service Bureaus and Agencies

More than fifteen hundred organizations now offer telemarketing services. Telemarketing service bureaus take or transfer phone orders and inquiries, while full-line telemarketing agencies can create, perform, and maintain complete telemarketing programs. Within service bureaus, dozens of communicators place or receive telephone calls all day long. These part-time or full-time personnel must have excellent communication skills and be friendly and personable.

Trainers, who instruct communicators about products and services and coach them in listening skills and sales techniques, are themselves supervised by the service bureau's managers. They monitor the output of bureau employees, measuring calls per hour, completed contacts per hour, and sales or orders per hour. When a service bureau provides both outbound and inbound services, there may be a manager or director for each division.

In telemarketing agencies, the service bureau is complemented by marketing-oriented staff who work with clients to develop programs; write, test, and revise scripts; select telephone lists; and evaluate results. Account executives organize and manage the client's program within the agency. In each of these positions, familiarity with the goals and processes of telemarketing is a must.

By the way, writers who develop telemarketing scripts rely on a different set of gifts than copywriters working with print. Because the telephone is an aural medium, a telephone script must "talk" easily, sound natural, and be easy to listen to and grasp over the phone.

Consumer Direct Marketers and Catalog Companies

Thanks to 800 numbers, the lion's share of goods and services ordered through direct marketing and catalog companies is placed by phone. Almost every direct marketing company offers an 800-number service now. When L.L. Bean, for many years a prominent hold-out, added an 800 number in 1986, telephone sales jumped to 70 percent of total catalog sales.

These companies use both inbound and outbound telemarketing to increase revenues. Customers who call to place orders can be told about short-term specials and related merchandise that, if added, can substantially increase the size of an order. Outbound telemarketing can be used to communicate with top customers, reactivate old ones, and, to some extent, prospect for new customers.

Business-to-Business Telemarketing and Telesales

In business-to-business environments, telemarketing is more accurately called "telesales." Here, selling takes place entirely by phone, instead of only partially, as is the case when a consumer is called a week or two after receiving a direct mail piece.

"Telesales is a hard business to do well in," Art Sobczak notes. "Someone who sells by phone must know a product or service inside and out—and be attuned to customer needs in order to find out how a business can benefit from the product or service. He or she also must be able to do both with less than half of the traditional communication tools. Telephone sales reps can't rely on the non-verbal or visual cues that are so important to sales professionals."

An inside sales representative must be able to:

- find out what a prospect's needs are in relation to the products or services the company is offering
- introduce appropriate products or services and outline their benefits to the listener
- conduct every step of the traditional sales process—including answering objections, probing for and overcoming resistance, and closing—by phone

Professional inside salespeople (as telesales representatives are also called) can make as much as outside salespeople who cover their territories in person. In fact, they can sometimes make more, because they can spend most of their time *selling* instead of driving between appointments, staying in hotels, sending in paperwork, and taking care of the details that plague the outside rep. In business-to-business telesales, compensation can begin at $60,000 a year. But in an environment in which the average sale is $1,240 (compared to $86 for the average consumer telephone sale), that's no surprise.

QUALIFICATIONS FOR TELEMARKETERS

People drawn to careers in telemarketing must be interested in people, eager to master telephone selling techniques, and have an aptitude for sales. "I'd say that sales aptitude is the most important quality," comments Joe Culotta, founder and owner of Telemarketing Search/Telemarketing Temps, the biggest broker of full-time and part-time telemarketing personnel in the United States. "The telephone is a sales channel, and it requires selling skills. More specifically, it takes a certain type to be able to sit down and sell by phone. Not everyone who has an aptitude for selling has an aptitude for selling by phone.

"Higher up the career ladder, managers need a comprehensive understanding of direct response marketing, marketing, and sales. They need to understand the essence of the medium in the same way that a pilot understands the essence of flying a plane or a doctor understands the essence of medicine."

SALARY RANGES

According to Connie Caroli, President of TeleManagement, a national executive search firm, wages in telemarketing will vary depending upon the environment. In a consumer telemarketing environment, where the average sale is small and communicators less skilled, salaries are lower. In a business-to-business environment, communicators may earn $70,000 a year. Supervisors' wages will be correspondingly higher.

At the first level are telephone communicators, who can make as little as $7.00 an hour or as much as $70,000 in salary and commissions a year. Above them are supervisors and trainers, who do not receive commissions; they coach communicators in selling technique and product knowledge, monitor and evaluate calls, and distribute the workload. A typical business-to-business supervisor oversees ten communicators; a consumer supervisor oversees twenty. Their pay can range from $28,000 to $35,000, with higher wages on the business-to-business side.

In large operations, telemarketing managers may manage as many as ten supervisors. They also may assume responsibility for operations, including staffing, distributing the calling hours and workload, gathering results data, and keeping statistics. Script writing is another duty. Telemarketing managers earn $46,000 to $70,000.

Telemarketing directors are involved in the overall direct marketing activities of a company. For them, telemarketing is but one channel in the overall marketing mix, although it is the channel in which they are experts. In a consumer in-house telemarketing center, telemarketing directors are responsible for the overall promotional campaign. In the business-to-business environment, they run the inside sales department. Salaries can range to $70,000 or more.

CHAPTER 7

THE LIST INDUSTRY

The success of every direct marketing enterprise depends on the strength of its customer and prospect lists. Even a package with a sure-fire offer and attention-getting graphics will bomb if it is sent to the wrong list.

A list represents a market segment—and there are many segments of the market in today's diverse society. Lists can reach everyone from gun enthusiasts to deep-sea divers, readers, antique collectors, opera season–ticket holders, sweepstakes respondents, computer analysts, millionaires, retired executives, and more.

Four kinds of lists are available for rent:

Compiled lists. Names compiled from telephone directories and other sources of public information, such as property transfer records, state driver's license bureaus, and voter registration records

Response lists. Lists of people who already have responded to an offer, such as people who purchased from The Sharper Image; subscribed to *Fortune* magazine; ordered flowers, steaks, fishing tackle, or wine by mail; or responded to an 800-number promotion. Consumer response lists contain names of consumers at home; business response lists consist of professionals at work.

House lists. A company's proprietary list of customers, which it uses for its own promotions and selectively rents out to companies with noncompeting offers. House lists can be huge. It's said that the house list for Fingerhut, the Minnesota direct marketing giant, is more than six million strong.

On-line lists. Opt-in e-mail lists consist mostly of people who have agreed to accept offers in areas of interest to them. Because no buying history accompanies the names, they are more akin to compiled than to response lists. Opt-in e-mail lists can be rented from a "dot-com" or on-line marketer. However, to honor the terms of the opt-in agreement, the renter's message must be "from" the list owner that customers gave permission to communicate. It's also difficult to run a merge-purge of such a list to eliminate duplication, in part because many people have more than one e-mail address. In 1999, on-line lists are available primarily from in-house list managers rather than brokers.

The people who buy, sell, manage, enhance, and recommend these lists comprise the mailing list industry. The main players are list brokers, list managers, list compilers, and the service bureaus that massage lists in an effort to increase their profitability and limit the waste created by mailing to the wrong names, expired addresses, or duplicates. Their clients are companies seeking to expand their customer bases by adding new names or generate revenues from their house lists through rental activities.

LIST BROKERS

List brokers match the marketers seeking new names with those list owners and managers who have lists for rent. A broker has no vested interest in any particular list, but sells his or her ability to find and recommend the "right" list for a particular venture. This entails researching and evaluating dozens of lists that at first glance appear to have little to do with the client's product or offer, but on a closer look may provide exactly the market segment a mailer is trying to reach.

For example, a good list broker would know that *Time* magazine subscribers, a largely upscale and aware audience, are a good list for a wide variety of fund-raising appeals.

List brokers help marketers select appropriate lists, plan mailings, analyze response, forecast response to future mailings, and will sometimes consult on a client's marketing strategy. They also must be familiar with segmentation and enhancement technology that adds demographic or psychographic detail to rental lists to help identify and break out the potentially profitable segments.

The entry-level job in the list brokerage business is *assistant account manager.* This person does lots of legwork: calling list owners for information about list characteristics and prices, researching lists, placing orders, following up on delivery, and handling invoice and billing problems. Although an assistant account manager communicates regularly with list owners and managers, he or she may not have as much contact with clients.

An *account manager* is responsible for the day-to-day service of a client account. He or she meets with clients, investigates their list needs, and then analyzes and recommends the lists that will help clients meet their revenue goals. Account managers must have a keen grasp of a client's market, so that they can assist clients in identifying new pools of prospects or expand existing pools. In addition, account managers help prospect for new clients for the brokerage firm.

Account managers and assistant account managers report to a *vice president/account supervisor,* who oversees the work of two to four subordinates while handling several major clients directly. New business prospecting is an additional duty.

Succeeding in the list brokerage business takes ambition, a love for markets and lists, an eye for detail, and strong oral and written communication skills. But a head for numbers is perhaps the most important quality of all.

"Direct marketing is a measurable business. Anyone looking for work in the list industry should have basic math skills, including a foundation in statistics," notes a list industry executive. "Our clients often give us the results of their most recent mailing and ask us to figure profit and loss for each of the lists they used. Based on those numbers, we then recommend which lists to continue to mail and which ones to drop. Even though clients can handle this analysis themselves, the trend is for people to ask brokers to handle it instead."

LIST MANAGERS

List managers rent lists to brokers or directly to mailers. As marketing consultants and salespeople, they are experts on the contents and the performance track record of the lists they manage.

List managers can work in-house or for a company that specializes in managing lists. Connie Howard, former list manager for CareerTrack, a Boulder, Colorado-based company that presents business seminars and sells audio and video tape programs on business skills, spent eight years handling the 2.5 million names on CareerTrack's list. When she first began, she was involved in every step of the process of promoting and renting CareerTrack's list: writing and proofing rate cards (which let potential renters know how much a thousand names cost, and what kind of "selects"—i.e., special segmentation options—are available), conducting sales presentations, designing promotions, fulfilling orders, invoicing renters, and overseeing the delivery of magnetic tapes and Cheshire label lists to clients. (Cheshire labels are gummed address labels printed on continuous forms, machine-cut, and machine-affixed to a mailing envelope.)

Eventually, she and her three associates rented approximately twenty-five million names annually. An expert on the characteristics of CareerTrack's house file, Howard was able to counsel potential clients on how to get the most of it. "Very few people can make all two million names work," she admits. "Our job was to help them find the targeted names on the file that would work for them."

To succeed in list management, Howard believes, "you need to understand what potential clients are looking for and make sure you offer as much added value as possible, through precise segmentation, demographic information, and top-notch customer service. To be really good, you need to have a passion for lists. It helps to really enjoy matching a mailer's offer to the most appropriate segment of your file. Of course, a list manager is fundamentally a salesperson—so your selling skills should be very strong.

"Intimate knowledge of a house file is an asset no matter what corner of direct marketing you want to move into. If you know your customer inside and out, you are better prepared to plan new products, devise marketing strategies, and pull together brilliant creative."

List managers who work for professional list management companies routinely handle several lists at a time. They promote the lists to prospective renters through promotions and rate cards, trade show exhibitions, advertisements in trade journals, and personal and telephone sales calls to brokers and list renters.

Often one company will offer both brokerage and management services through two separately operating divisions. The Kleid Company's management division represents about one hundred lists, including the subscriber lists of Condé Nast magazines. Each of its *account representatives* handles a group of lists that ranges from five to fifteen. These account reps handle all contact with list owners and serve as resources to brokers and mailers who call for information about the content, characteristics, and performance of the lists. They know how a list was generated, who is on it, what kind of offers it has been successfully used for, and how it can be segmented.

Assistant account representatives support the account representatives by processing orders, coordinating delivery, and preparing orders for billing.

Sales managers or *sales directors* sell managed lists to brokers and mailers and handle presentations to list owners searching for a management firm.

A *vice president/account supervisor* oversees the work of these lower-level employees and also handles high-level client contact. At the very top, a general manager runs the list management operations and, if the division is part of a combined brokerage/management company, reports to the principals or president of the entire company.

At The Kleid Company, a *financial specialist* handles earnings projections for prospective clients who are interested in discovering what their lists are likely to earn in a year. He or she also runs the numbers for current clients, who receive an annual projection of rental income.

Although Kleid works with an agency to produce promotional material for the lists it manages, other agencies have in-house creative staff. They write space advertisements, sales letters, and direct mail brochures that promote the lists to the trade.

LIST COMPILERS

The list compilation business was born in 1947, when Rose Rashmir hired women in Redlands, California, to type labels directly from telephone and municipal directories for a national list of potential customers for the Diners Club.

Today list compilers continue to develop lists by capturing data from a variety of commercial and public sources, although lists and labels are no longer typed by hand! Information on consumers is compiled from telephone directories, voter registration lists, automobile registrations, and other public information. Information on businesses is often obtained from professional organizations or trade show attendees.

Large compilers have databases with marketing-oriented information on millions of individuals and households in more than ten thousand compiled lists. This information is often enhanced through demographic information that can add data about sex, income, age, family size, car ownership, telephone number, and neighborhood demographics to a simple name and address file.

List compilers require the services of data processors, computer programmers, program analysts, software engineers, and sales representatives. It takes the work of detail-oriented professionals to keep the lists up to date (a problem, since the public records on which these lists are based are sometimes a year old before they are published) and marketable.

SERVICE BUREAUS

Service bureaus were introduced on the heels of the Zip Code in 1963, when mailers needed someone to organize, maintain, and presort lists in Zip Code order to take advantage of new postal service discounts and incentives. Over the years, service bureaus also began to offer merge-purge services, which combine two or more lists into one to identify and/or eliminate duplicate names.

Today, service bureaus can help a mailer segment lists by geography, income, and other characteristics; they also can analyze response, offer sophisticated demographic data overlays that add meaning to a list, and convert lists to Cheshire labels or magnetic tapes. Some offer list management services that help mailers add, delete, or alter names and records on a house list.

Some service bureaus are taking on the look and feel of database consultants and now offer cutting-edge data processing, analyzing, and modeling techniques. That's why personnel in service bureaus must have a very good grasp of computer and technical skills, including statistical analysis. Even salespeople need to understand the technical side, in order to credibly sell their services to brokers, managers, and mailers.

MOBILITY IN THE LIST INDUSTRY

Knowledge of a list—or more than one—is a great asset to a career in direct marketing. "Once you become a list specialist, you can be in demand on both the brokerage/management side or the client side. Lots of direct marketing companies are looking for list specialists," says Richard Vergara of the Kleid Company. As for getting started in the business, he observes that, "the ideal way to break into the list business is to start out on the client side and learn how to put a mailing together. That hands-on experience will pay off in the brokerage business."

According to Richard Vergara, it is more common for people to move from list brokerage into list management for a management company or a client than it is for list managers to become list brokers. "The skills of list brokers are a little more specific."

SALARY RANGES

Anyone interested in entering the mailing list industry must have a head for numbers and an ability to plan and analyze. Also helpful are good oral and written communication skills and basic knowledge of computer programs like Lotus.

List brokerage firms

Professional list brokers earn commission on top of a base salary. The base salary can be as little as $30,000—but the sky's the limit for brokers who produce.

List management firms

Assistant account representative	$30,000–40,000
Account representative	$35,000–55,000
Sales manager	$50,000+
Vice president/account supervisor	$70,000+

List compilers and service bureaus

Wages in these two areas are roughly similar to wages in list management.

Entry-level personnel	$28,000–35,000
Mid-level personnel	$35,000–45,000
Management	$45,000–50,000
Senior management	$60,000+

CHAPTER 8

DATABASE MARKETING

Database technology and digital media are driving marketers to shift away from mass-marketing techniques that reach very large segments and embrace highly targeted techniques instead.

Rather than selling one product to everyone, marketers now develop "niche" products that appeal to small segments of the population. But communicating with these groups can be a challenge, since the proliferation of niche magazines, television and cable networks, mailing lists, and newspapers have left advertisers with no single "mass" medium that can efficiently reach them.

What's the result? Marketers and advertisers are seeking other channels for product promotion. Cigarette marketers are searching for them with real urgency, as more and more advertising media are closed to them. Many of these companies are learning to cultivate a tremendously effective private promotional channel: database marketing.

The direct marketing agency Kobs, Gregory & Passavant defines database marketing as:

> Marketing to individual, known customers or prospects, using purchase history and lifestyle data to target relevant offers and rewards that increase response or brand loyalty more efficiently than other media alternatives.

Databases help collect information on the habits and preferences of customers and prospects—information that can help a marketer sell products that match a customer's particular taste. Using a database of customers whose demographic, income, and lifestyle characteristics accompany their purchasing history, a company can design powerful offers that address the ultimate target: an individual consumer. By linking the database to the Internet, direct marketers can create messages and offers that are relevant to specific segments of the population one person at a time.

BENEFITS AND APPLICATIONS OF DATABASE MARKETING

An efficiently maintained database can accomplish a number of marketing goals. It can be used to:

- generate and track leads for salespeople
- identify and test opportunities for new products, services, and businesses
- track the effectiveness of advertising among longtime or newly acquired customers
- cross-sell existing products to current customers
- construct a profile of current customers, enabling a company to identify potential new customers who resemble that profile
- identify and predict purchasing trends
- personalize marketing communications to customers

Some of these applications—like tracking the effectiveness of advertising—can be executed with a "historical" database of customer purchase records. But database marketing generally entails taking an internal, historical database and adding outside information to it, to learn facts about customers or prospects that can't be generated internally. This extra layer of information is needed whenever *predictive* data—projected sales trends or response rates, for example—are desired.

SOURCES OF INFORMATION

In today's marketplace, information about consumers is easy to come by. The major sources are government census data, auto registrations and driver's licenses, telephone directory information, and data culled from responses to warranty cards and consumer surveys. All are captured by companies that specialize in providing demographic and psychographic information about American consumers. A company like Donnelley Marketing, for example, has information on more than eighty-five million households. Its customers can target the consumers they wish to reach by overlaying lifestyle data on their own customer records.

Demographic and psychographic information is available at three levels:

- Zip Code or census tract level
- Zip-Plus-Four level, corresponding to a single residential block or building
- household or individual level

At the household or individual level, "one-on-one marketing" is slowly becoming a reality, as marketers learn enough about a household to make an individualized pitch economically feasible. But what is clearly an unparalleled opportunity for marketers nevertheless makes other people nervous. U.S. legislatures have enacted laws to protect consumer privacy, and some European countries have national agencies overseeing the uses of personal information. As database technology and digital media create reservoirs of on-line information, interest is growing in rules that would inform people about how information is collected and used.

Whether database marketing gains momentum or is stopped in its tracks depends a great deal on how responsibly consumer information is used. It is up to direct and database marketers to apply consumer information in a way that is welcomed, not feared.

DATABASE CAREER OPPORTUNITIES

Every chapter of this book has discussed database opportunities, albeit briefly. That's because database marketing is an increasingly important part of direct marketing. There are even those who predict that *database marketing* will eventually replace *direct marketing* as the term for both the industry and the technique.

While positions such as data analyst, programmer, or database manager require a statistical or computer programming background, there are many jobs in the database field that are not technical at all. And although it is important to understand available technology and have a basic grasp of analysis and modeling techniques, a knowledge of the range of data sources and very sharp marketing skills is even more essential.

Until recently, database technology outpaced database applications. But as companies rush to link their house files to an e-commerce site, more marketers are carving out new applications for database-driven marketing and creative programs. People who offer a blend of analytical skills, data knowledge, and marketing sense are hard to find, however. "When we needed to hire someone to run our U.K. office's database consulting division, we interviewed seventy-three candidates before we found one person with the background we wanted," says one executive.

Today positions in database marketing are available in:

- "dot-coms" of all kinds
- direct marketing and catalog companies
- package goods companies
- banks and financial services firms
- direct marketing agencies
- data collection companies
- management consulting firms
- database agencies
- software companies and database vendors

Let's examine each one.

"Dot-Coms"

"Companies didn't need database marketing in the traditional world, but they can't do without it in the web world," says database expert Rob Jackson. Every on-line transaction generates customer information, and every dot-com needs people with database savvy to take those names and demographic data and use them to create additional business.

"Dot-coms" use the database to:

- capture customer names and data and manage those names effectively
- integrate customer information from many web sites
- identify high-value customers and create loyalty programs to keep them coming back
- segment customers into target markets and develop relationship marketing programs for specific targets or even individuals
- use statistical analysis to find correlations among existing buyers and develop profiles of prospects who are likely to purchase in the future

Direct Marketing and Catalog Companies

Direct marketing and catalog companies have access to a great deal of transaction-based information. Whenever a customer orders a pair of waders from L.L. Bean, for example, the details of that purchase—quantity, color, size, method of payment—are recorded. Astute marketers can use these customer records to study marketing trends and refine selling approaches.

Data specialists who maintain and massage in-house files can extract information that helps focus and improve company marketing strategies. A product manager or a merchandise manager may ask data specialists to compare the profiles of two different types of customers in order to determine how best to sell to each one. Direct marketing firms also can use their databases to:

- communicate with and activate inactive buyers
- send special promotions to their best buyers
- remind purchasers of bulk products to order again
- thank customers for orders, send "anniversary mailings" that acknowledge their tenure as customers, and help maintain a steady communication between company and customers

Package Goods Companies

As the mass market declines, even package goods companies are catching database fever. For decades they were content knowing a great deal about the market segments that purchased their products but very little about the individuals who made the purchase decisions. Today many of the biggest companies are actively collecting consumer names and constructing marketing programs to attract new buyers and reward loyal users.

Major marketers like Procter & Gamble are using their databases to

- welcome new customers
- convert nonusers and competitive users to customers
- increase the purchase frequency of light users
- reward heavy users

Cigarette makers are relying heavily on databases now that broadcast advertising is no longer allowed and a ban on print cigarette advertising is being considered. Using coupon offers, they are building large databases of smokers with whom they can communicate. This cost-effective "private marketplace" can be reached without wasting effort on nonsmokers. Promotions to the database also can be conducted without immediately alerting competing brands, as coupon campaigns in magazines and newspapers inevitably do.

Banks and Financial Services Firms

Banks and financial services companies, such as credit card marketers, insurance companies, and investment groups, accumulate sensitive financial data in the process of conducting their business. This valuable information must be used with discretion. Merrill Lynch, for example, allows its brokers to use client financial information in-house, but it does not allow its use in mailings for fear of offending clients who may feel that confidentiality has been betrayed.

But banks are using their transaction files to set up all types of direct marketing programs. Some identify the services that a customer is or is not using, so that other services can be cross-sold through direct mail promotions or e-mail messages to on-line banking customers. Other banks are tracking the dates on which large deposits, such as paychecks or bonuses, are made and designing mail promotions for CDs, mutual funds, and other investments that will arrive just before the big check is deposited.

Direct Marketing Agencies

As direct marketing agencies are asked to consult on database strategy, they are hiring personnel with database expertise.

For example, Leo Burnett maintains a significant database group to provide clients with strategic advice on how to grow and get more from a database. In some instances, Burnett clients who don't want to maintain an in-house database have asked Burnett to locate a qualified vendor who can manage the database and help them understand how to use it. Another major direct marketing agency provides a full range of information management services. Its staff can assist in building a database from the ground up or examine a client's database and recommend new ventures or businesses it can launch.

Data Collection Companies

Two major players in the data collection field—R.L. Polk and Donnelley Marketing—started out by publishing city address and telephone directories. Over the years, these directories have evolved into electronic databases that contain information about almost every household in the United States. Metromail is another large vendor of information data.

Not so coincidentally, these three companies are also the nation's largest list compilers. Why the overlap? Because thanks to computers, the lists they make available for rental also can be used to enhance a database.

The other major data collection agencies are the three major credit-reporting agencies: TRW, Equifax, and Trans Union Corp. Logically, each one has access to the sensitive financial information about U.S. consumers prized by marketers.

Management Consulting Firms

Because they began as accounting firms, major management consulting firms such as Andersen Consulting and Ernst and Young were already involved in finance and data processing. Moving into database management and consulting was a natural extension for these companies, which hire analysts, programmers, and marketing strategists to work with clients in an effort to maximize profits from a database.

Database Agencies

Database agencies, such as Epsilon and MARC, are marketing-driven rather than technology-driven. Although they can offer data management, statistical analysis, and modeling, and although they rely on up-to-date technology to do so, they focus on offering strategic marketing and creative advice. These agencies can create, execute, and manage a database marketing program.

Software Companies and Database Vendors

Database vendors selling the file formats on which databases are constructed, and software companies writing the application programs that let users access information, need technical people to develop their products and sales representatives to market them.

One rep who has sold both hardware and software notes that "sales representatives must understand the technical specifications of their product or service, as well as the needs of the company they are calling on. Most of these companies also employ consultants who help end users design and install a system so it generates the results they want. Both consultants and sales representatives must work with users to make sure the system or software fits the company's needs. If it doesn't, it quickly becomes 'shelfware'— software or applications that cannot be used because they were done improperly or are no longer needed when finished."

A CAREER IN DATABASE MARKETING:
ROB JACKSON

When Rob Jackson started his career in database marketing, the field didn't even have a name.

After graduating with a degree in marketing, he cut his teeth in advertising and promotion as an agency account executive on the national Burger Chef account. After three years, he left the agency and moved to ITT Educational Services, a chain of schools that offers post-high school training in fields like auto mechanics and electronics. There he helped design and implement a marketing campaign that attracted new students to the programs offered by the schools. By generating new leads for each program and tracking how many new students actually enrolled in the program, Jackson, in effect, ran a database-driven enrollment program.

Next came a stint at Wickes Corporation, a manufacturer of pole-frame buildings like garages and auto dealerships. As ad manager for the building division, he developed a program to generate business for fifty company-owned branches. Again, a database was used to capture information about prospects and track the percentage of conversion to sales.

After two direct marketing jobs and a stint in a sales promotion agency, Rob and a partner created Integrated Target Marketing. Their company's goal was to use customer information to drive marketing programs for both consumer and business-to-business clients. After three and a half years in business, he decided to go out on his own as a consultant. Trying to drum up business, he approached May & Speh, a database company that was using Integrated Target Marketing's services. May & Speh refused to hire him as a consultant—but offered to take him on full-time.

"It never occurred to me to join that kind of business," says Rob, "but I was tired of meeting payroll and shouldering all the obligations that go with the territory in a small business." After working at May & Speh, Rob moved to Donnelley Marketing.

Several positions later, Rob became Marketing Director for Donnelley Marketing, where he helped companies use customer information to drive marketing programs for both consumer and business-to-business clients. While Executive Vice President and General Manager of Customer Management Services, which specialized in database marketing for telecommunications, financial services, utilities, and health care, he restructured and merged the company with two others to create Knowledge-Based Marketing, now a part of Young and Rubicam advertising.

Today Rob is a principal of Dialogos, a database consulting firm that provides a portfolio of services. Among the services they offer, Rob and his people:

1. develop data warehouses that integrate marketing and sales tools and develop and manage web sites
2. use data and customer modeling to provide business intelligence and optimization
3. consult with companies on management and organizational structure and strategic business planning
4. design integrated marketing programs
5. develop e-commerce and e-marketing programs

"Database technology has the capacity to change everything about the way a company works," Rob says. "Dialogos staff can build and implement databases and help a company alter its structure to match the new way of doing business."

Nearly every Dialogos client wants help with e-commerce. For example, after helping the toy company, Hasbro, consolidate its many separate databases into one customer database, Dialogos trained Hasbro employees to capture customer names and data, showed them how to manage those names effectively, and helped them develop relationship marketing programs that communicate and sell more product to customers. Many of the relationship marketing programs are conducted through the fifty web sites that support Hasbro's software, collectibles, Star Wars toys, and other products. A web site for the popular Furbies has as many as two million hits a week—all potential customers for the company.

Before the advent of e-commerce, a company could survive without database marketing, but that is no longer true. "On the web, interactions happen more quickly and are more complex," Rob explains. "Without sophisticated database marketing tools, it can't be done."

Ironically, Rob finds himself dispensing basic direct marketing advice to young people whose technical skills are superb but who know little about direct marketing. "They're amazed to discover that the strategies for writing effective, motivating copy that were invented and tested long ago apply directly to the web environment," he says.

"In essence, we have taken what we've learned over the years, and through database applications have integrated sales forces, marketing departments, customers, and creative into a powerful marketing force."

SALARY RANGES

Junior analysts who perform the computer programs that drive database marketing and *data sourcers* who source data earn between $40,000 and $50,000. *Senior analysts* earn $50,000 to $80,000, although those capable of performing sophisticated modeling functions on state-of-the-art software can command $80,000 to $150,000.

Database managers who manage programs for major marketers earn between $75,000 and $150,000, and some stars in the field earn a great deal more. *Database consultants* can earn upwards of $150,000.

CHAPTER 9

OPPORTUNITIES IN OTHER INDUSTRIES

The technique of direct marketing is the tool of choice in many surprising fields, from banking, insurance, and other financial service organizations to package goods and retail. In fact, some non-direct marketing companies are the real pacesetters in using database marketing and the Internet to establish a dialogue between customers and the company. Another source of jobs in direct marketing comes from suppliers to the industry, such as printers and lettershops.

This chapter looks at other fields in which direct marketing skills are important.

PACKAGE GOODS MARKETERS

Even old-line product managers at companies like Procter & Gamble are mastering and deploying direct marketing techniques along with the traditional techniques they use to build consumer awareness and brand usage.

It's largely the database that is responsible for these changes in technique. Its ability to store and use accurate and extensive historical information on customers, coupled with its ability to immediately measure the results of any marketing program, make database marketing an indispensable tool of product and marketing managers in dozens of fields. Databases help these professionals focus on specific consumer market segments...even on specific consumers!

A database developed from coupons redeemed by consumers of a particular breakfast cereal, for example, could be used to:

- mail special promotions to current users of the brand
- mail discounts offering more savings to people who eat other similar cereals
- offer coupons on other products in the brand "family"
- mail special merchandise offers to users
- send a newsletter to users
- test new products related to the "flagship" product

In *Profitable Direct Marketing,* Jim Kobs points out that package goods manufacturers also can use direct marketing to profitably sell products that are retail "misfits," such as oversize garbage bags that aren't stocked in the supermarket, but are promoted in inserts in the regular-size boxes so people can order them by mail. Direct marketing also can help strengthen markets that are underperforming, by targeting direct marketing programs to lower-selling regions to pull the product through the distribution channel.

INSURANCE AND OTHER FINANCIAL SERVICES

Actually, insurance direct marketing hardly qualifies as an "other" industry. Many of the largest direct marketing companies are either exclusively in the insurance business or have insurance divisions.

During the Depression, companies like Allstate and Equitable Life Assurance began offering life, accident, and auto policies by mail. More and more followed suit, until today almost every major insurance company—even those with very large agency forces and sales office networks—participates in direct marketing.

Some of them use direct marketing to produce leads that are then distributed or sold to their agents. Others develop insurance policies exclusively for sale by mail, simplifying the qualification process and the application form so that the offer can be made in an appealing and creative way. Still others rent lists of customers and prospects from their agents and use these lists to sell policies that the agents would never bother with because commissions are too low.

Agents and brokers, at first threatened by what they perceived to be competition, have made peace with mail-order insurance and are exploring how they can apply direct marketing to their own books of business. Now large and small agencies are learning how to generate and convert leads using direct mail and telemarketing and how to track customers on databases so that they can develop targeted mailings to coincide with birthdays, policy expiration dates, and other events that can bring in new business.

Credit cards, debit cards, consumer loans, mutual fund investments—all are successfully marketed through direct marketing. People who respond to the mailings enjoy the convenience of reviewing the offers in the privacy of their own homes and often are pleased to be able to purchase them without having to deal with an agent.

FINANCIAL INSTITUTIONS

Banks and savings and loans understand that the financial records they maintain for their customers can assist their marketing efforts. They now are asking their marketing staffs to learn how to recruit new accounts, sign up new prospects for loans, and even approve small loans by mail or phone.

Upon discovering that a major corporation planned to move to its community, one Alabama bank developed a campaign that blended direct marketing and public relations to recruit the banking business of the relocating employees. It sent new-account applications, along with extensive community information and a personalized letter to each of the employees, and successfully recruited 75 percent of the accounts of families relocating to the town.

THE AUTOMOBILE INDUSTRY

Direct marketing is even cropping up in the automobile industry. Porsche has used direct marketing to promote its deluxe cars. A two-page letter—printed on watermarked stationery for a simple, classic look—urged three hundred thousand high-income prospects to visit a dealer and take a test drive. In this lead-generation program, the primary emphasis fell on defining and then locating qualified prospects. Porsche didn't want to alienate dealers by sending in people who wanted to test drive but couldn't truly afford the car.

Another car maker tracked purchasers of one of its models and sent "time to buy a new car" reminders to owners five years later. Even car dealers are using databases and direct marketing to promote maintenance and repair services and to put their dealerships first in line when their customers start looking for a new car.

RETAIL

Retail stores are using direct and interactive marketing as a separate sales channel and to build store traffic. Major chains like

Bloomingdale's and Neiman-Marcus offer catalogs of high-priced, specialty goods whose sales equal or surpass those of their best stores. Major catalogers like Eddie Bauer are going the opposite way, setting up retail outlets to complement their catalog sales. In all, it's estimated that about a third of all consumer mail-order sales are generated by retailers with mail-order divisions.

Retailers also use direct marketing to build traffic and sales for existing stores. Body Works designs its catalog to encourage store visits as well as direct orders. Gordon's Alley, a men's clothing store, established a Gold Card program for its best customers, who receive monthly personalized mailings that generate strong sales.

Catalog retail chains follow the same strategy. Eddie Bauer and other retailers know that a sizable number of their catalogs will not be used for direct mail shopping, but rather for background on purchases that will ultimately be made in their stores. At one time, research by Sears showed that families who received Sears catalogs were twice as likely to shop in a Sears store than those who did not see the catalog. Better yet, catalog recipients spent twice as much as others on in-store sales.

Finally, retailers are launching catalogs in order to establish and strengthen a presence on the web. A paper catalog can tell customers where and how to find you and include special incentives that drive sales to the Internet.

MAGAZINE SUBSCRIPTION CIRCULATION

Most magazine subscriptions are sold through the mail and fulfilled by mail. Therefore, magazine subscriptions are a direct mail business, and jobs in circulation are jobs in direct marketing.

When a new magazine concept is tested, its creators first identify its likely audience by studying lists of people with profiles similar to the new magazine's "ideal" subscriber. Next, they test-mail a subscription offer to those lists. Because they must persuade people to become readers of a magazine no one has ever seen, these packages feature long copy and elaborate brochures describing the magazine's content. If response warrants it, the magazine is published and subscription campaigns are conducted in earnest.

Established magazines like *Time* and *Rolling Stone* must seek new readers as well as retain old ones. Renewal letters tend to be shorter but are sent more frequently. A publisher may send six or seven renewal reminders before it writes off a subscriber.

The famous sweepstakes contests of Publishers Clearing House and American Family Publishers are used to acquire new subscribers, although they are often not good prospects for renewal.

Magazine publishers are also in the list business, because their subscribers represent substantial rental income. Most publishers employ list managers to promote their lists to appropriate noncompeting marketers.

FUND-RAISING

For decades, nonprofit organizations have turned to the mail and the telephone to solicit modest contributions. Even large donors are often "warmed up" with a personal letter before being contacted in person.

In recent years, nonprofits have been turning to the Internet to raise public awareness about their causes and to tackle limited fund-raising. Using a web site to provide up-to-the-minute news and photos about natural and political disasters spreads the word about a nonprofit's mission to an audience beyond current donors; adding a response mechanism encourages donations from visitors to the site. Others may visit a web site and later make a donation by phone or mail. Opt-in e-mail messages to current donors and site visitors helped the Red Cross raise a million dollars for the crisis in Kosovo.

Fund-raising writers need to be able to convey a sense of urgency, as well as a sense of guilt about not responding...and a sense of satisfaction for those who do. And fund-raising media specialists need to be quite creative when identifying pools of new donors. Large nonprofit organizations may employ a cadre of fund-raising direct marketing specialists, although most turn to direct marketing agencies (including some that specialize in fund-raising) for assistance.

BROADCAST DIRECT MARKETING

While most prime-time television commercials are image advertisements, many non-prime-time spots are direct marketing ads. These are an outgrowth of the live commercials of the 1950s, when pitchmen who could sell anything to anybody used language, posture, gestures, expressions, and props to sell food slicers, juicers, fishing kits, miracle cleaners, knives, and other products. Back in the 1950s, these commercials were so popular that they were listed in TV schedules, and on at least one occasion a commercial for Salad Maker drew higher ratings than the Lawrence Welk show.

Agencies like A. Eicoff & Company specialize in broadcast direct marketing. Its founder, Al Eicoff, notes that the key to making a sale through a broadcast direct response commercial is to make the sale as easy as possible. His motto is "tease 'em, please 'em, seize 'em." "You tease the viewer by raising his expectations. You promise the viewer a product that is better and more useful than anything he's ever seen. You please him with the demonstration of the product—a demonstration that has an almost visceral fascination. And, finally, you seize him with the offer; an offer so attractive that ordering the product seems like a perfectly logical thing to do."

VENDORS TO THE DIRECT MARKETING INDUSTRY

Lettershops

Lettershops are the organizations that get mail campaigns into the mail. Although many jobs are mechanical or clerical in nature, each one is absolutely essential to "dropping" a campaign, especially one that contains several different components.

Lettershop sales personnel consult with clients (direct marketing companies or agencies), specifying requirements for insertion and labeling and confirming the number of mailing pieces that will be needed to complete the mailing. Under their supervision, lettershop personnel can:

- fold and collate packages
- code order forms and labels
- prepare the mailing for the post office
- follow up with written reports that confirm receipt of materials, mailing costs, and drop dates

Some lettershops also can handle list maintenance and processing, as well as printing.

On the client side, large direct marketing companies sometimes have a lettershop coordinator who manages the multiple mailings going out of multiple lettershops.

Print Production Suppliers

Behind every great direct marketing package is a talented printer. And working for that printer is a host of sales and customer service professionals who nurse complicated, multicomponent mailings from final mechanicals to finished piece. In a very real sense, they are equal partners to the companies and agencies they serve, the vendor counterpart to the production specialists on the client side.

The best graphic arts professionals understand not only the technical aspects of printing a job, but also the dimensions of the direct marketing business. That's why many of them join local direct marketing clubs and work hard to stay abreast of trends in direct marketing. That's also why their work is honored by ECHO and other industry awards, which recognize that a great creative execution needs a flawless printing job to succeed.

Opportunities for aspiring art directors abound at many vendors, who often employ keyliners, desktop publishing specialists, and creative staff.

CHAPTER 10

EDUCATIONAL PREPARATION AND INTERNSHIP OPPORTUNITIES

Programs that specialize in direct marketing have taken root at colleges and universities around the country, and a rich variety of professional courses is also offered through the Direct Marketing Association, the Canadian Direct Marketing Association, and regional direct marketing clubs throughout the country. Even a single course can help orient you to the field; multiple courses or a certificate will give you a thorough grounding in direct marketing and increase your value to a prospective employer.

U.S. COLLEGES AND UNIVERSITIES

For a complete list of colleges and universities offering degree, diploma, and certificate programs in direct marketing, visit the Direct Marketing Educational Foundation (DMEF) web site (www.the-dma.org/dmef). In addition, more than 260 colleges and universities throughout the United States offer individual courses on direct marketing. Contact the DMEF for details at 212/ 768–7277, extension 1817.

Degree, Certificate, and Specialization Programs

Baruch College
School of Business
City University of New York
New York, NY 10010

Baruch's undergraduate School of Business offers a B.B.A. in Marketing with a twenty-four-credit Direct Marketing track.

Bentley College
Division of Continuing Education
175 Forest Street
Room 220, Morison Hall
Waltham, MA 02154-4705

Offers a Certificate in Direct Marketing endorsed by the New England Direct Marketing Association, whose members serve as faculty.

California State University, Bakersfield
School of Business & Public Administration
Bakersfield, CA 93311-1099

Offers a Direct Marketing Certificate Program.

California State University, Fullerton
Marketing Department
School of Business Administration
Fullerton, CA 92634
www.fullerton.edu (click on extended education)

Offers a seven-course Certificate in Direct Marketing co-sponsored by the Department of Marketing, the School of Business Administration, and the Direct Marketing Association of Orange County.

DePaul University
Vachel Pennebaker Certificate in Direct Marketing
DePaul Center
One East Jackson Boulevard
Chicago, IL 60604-2287

A comprehensive twenty-week program supported by the Chicago Association of Direct Marketing's Educational Foundation, the Pennebaker Certificate focuses on interactive marketing. Also offers an annual Executive Forum series that covers special direct marketing topics.

Emory University
Center for Relationship Marketing
1602 Mizell Drive
Atlanta, GA 30322

Offers special programs as well as an M.B.A. in Relationship Marketing; both university faculty and industry executives serve as program leaders and facilitators.

Fashion Institute of Technology
Room B403
Seventh Avenue at 27th Street
New York, NY 10001-5992
www.fitnyc.suny.edu

Offers a B.S. degree in Direct Marketing.

Ferris State University
251 Plymouth SE
Grand Rapids, MI 49506

Offers a twelve-credit Direct Marketing Certificate.

Florida Gulf Coast University
College of Business Marketing
10501FBCU Boulevard South
Fort Myers, FL 33965-6565
www.fgcu.edu/cob/mkt

Offers a Specialization in Interactive Marketing.

James Madison University
College of Business
Marketing Department, MSC 0205
Harrisonburg, VA 22807

Offers a Concentration in Market Information Systems.

Johnson & Wales University
Fashion & Retail Management
8 Abbott Park Place
Providence, RI 02903

Offers a Direct Response Retailing program that uses course work and internships to prepare students in storefront retailing and catalog development and operations.

Loyola University
Marketing Department
820 North Michigan Avenue
Chicago, IL 60611

Offers an M.S. degree in Integrated Marketing Communications.

Mercy College
Direct Marketing Program
555 Broadway
Dobbs Ferry, NY 10522

Offers an M.S. degree in Direct Marketing and an eight-month specialization/certificate program that can be earned in the class-room or via the Internet.

Merrimack College
Center for Direct Marketing
315 Turnpike Street
208 O'Reilly Hall
North Andover, MA 01845

Offers a Direct Marketing Certificate Program comprised of six core evening courses and five optional professional development day seminars. Also offers undergraduate credit courses in direct marketing.

Milwaukee Area Technical College
700 West State Street
Milwaukee, WI 53233

Awards an Advanced Technical Certificate for completion of four direct marketing courses and a principles of marketing course. Courses also may be taken for credit toward an associate degree.

New York University
The Center for Direct Marketing
New York University School of Continuing Education and
    Professional Studies
11 West Forty-second Street, Room 401
New York, NY 10003

Offers a thirty-eight-credit M.S. degree in Direct Marketing
Communication along with noncredit evening courses in a variety
of direct and interactive subjects.

Northern Illinois University
Marketing Department
DeKalb, IL 60115

Offers an area of study in direct marketing that is supported by the
Chicago Association of Direct Marketing's Educational Foundation.

Northwestern University
Integrated Marketing Communications
Medill School of Journalism
1908 Sheridan Road
Evanston, IL 60208

Direct marketing and e-commerce are merged in the Integrated
Marketing Communications graduate program, which requires
sixteen courses, a summer residency at a data-driven direct marketing company, and a practicum in electronic commerce.

Oakton Community College
Marketing Department
1600 East Golf Road
Des Plaines, IL 60016

Offers a two-year Associate degree in Direct Marketing and a
twelve-hour certificate program.

Pennsylvania State University
Department of Marketing
Smeal College of Business Administration
701 Business Administration Building
University Park, PA 16802-3007

Offers a four-course Direct Marketing Certificate.

Regis University
School of Professional Studies
3333 Regis Boulevard, Mailcode K-8
Denver, CO 80221

Offers a thirty-week Direct Marketing Certificate Program in conjunction with the Rocky Mountain Direct Marketing Association.

Roosevelt University
Walter E. Heller College of Business Administration
430 South Michigan Avenue
Chicago, IL 60605-1394

Offers an M.S. degree in Integrated Marketing Communications that integrates direct marketing into most areas of marketing communications.

University of California, Berkeley
Extension
CEBM-2223 Fulton Street
Berkeley, CA 94720

Offers a four-course, 120-hour Study Program in Direct Marketing.

University of Cincinnati
Direct Marketing Policy Center
431 Carl Lindner Hall
Mail Location 145
Cincinnati, OH 45221-0145

Sponsors undergraduate instruction, student internships, an M.B.A., and a range of management seminars, but does not offer a degree program.

University of Colorado
School of Journalism and Mass Communication
Campus Box 287
Boulder, CO 80309

Offers an M.A. degree in Integrated Marketing Communications.

University of Kentucky
Journalism Department
107 Grehan Building
Lexington, KY 40506-0042

Offers an Integrated Strategic Communication major with a Direct Response path.

University of Massachusetts
Marketing Department
Isenberg School of Management
Amherst, MA 01003

Offers an undergraduate specialization in e-commerce and technology that combines direct marketing with database, MIS, and computer science courses.

University of Missouri
Center for Direct Marketing Education and Research
Henry Bloch School of Business and Public Administration
5100 Rockhill Road
Kansas City, MO 64110-2499

Offers an M.B.A. degree with a concentration in Marketing/ Direct Marketing as well as a three-week residential certificate program for practitioners. Successful completion leads to the designation P.D.M., Professional Direct Marketer.

University of Texas
Advertising Department
CMA7.142
Austin, TX 78712

Offers a B.S., M.A., and Ph.D. in Advertising that includes integrated, interactive, and direct marketing and communication.

Virginia Commonwealth University
Department of Marketing and Business Law
1015 Floyd Avenue
Richmond, VA 23284-4000

Offers a Certified Direct Marketer (C.D.M.) Program consisting of eight two-day, weekend modules that cover key areas of direct marketing.

Walsh College
3838 Livernois
Troy, MI 48065

Offers a major, a certificate program, and a specialization in interactive marketing in the classroom or via the Internet. The Certification Program is endorsed by the Great Lakes Marketing Association.

Western Connecticut State University
Certificate Program in Direct Marketing
Marketing Department
Danbury, CT 06810

Offers a two-semester Certificate Program in Direct Marketing as well as an undergraduate concentration in Interactive Marketing.

CANADIAN COLLEGES AND UNIVERSITIES

Contact the Canadian Marketing Association (www.the-cma.org) for complete information on direct marketing programs offered at these postsecondary institutions.

Acadia University
Wolfville, Nova Scotia

Assiniboine Community College
Brandon, Manitoba

British Columbia Institute of Technology
Burnaby, British Columbia

Canadore College
North Bay, Ontario

Centennial College
Toronto, Ontario

Conestoga College
Kitchener, Ontario

Confederation College
Thunder Bay, Ontario

Dalhousie University
Halifax, Nova Scotia

Durham College
Whitby, Ontario

Georgian College
Owen Sound, Ontario

Humber College
Etobicoke, Ontario

Mohawk College
Hamilton, Ontario

Sheridan College
Brampton, Ontario

Simon Fraser University
Vancouver, British Columbia

Sir Sanford Fleming College
Peterborough, Ontario

St. Lawrence College
Kingston, Ontario

University of Toronto
Toronto, Ontario

York University
Toronto, Ontario

YOUR BEST SOURCE: THE DIRECT MARKETING
EDUCATIONAL FOUNDATION

The Direct Marketing Educational Foundation is dedicated to teaching students about direct marketing and encouraging them to choose direct marketing as a career. It's a terrific clearinghouse of opportunities for learning about the field. Through its programs, it spreads the word about direct marketing among the young. And by making the resumes of its program graduates available to the direct marketing companies that help sponsor it, the DMEF also helps spread the word about talented young job-seekers. Whether you are researching direct marketing or gearing up for a full-press job search, the DMEF should be your first stop. The DMEF is located at 1120 Avenue of the Americas, New York, NY 10036-6700. Access the DMEF's web site at www.the-dma.org/dmef.

DMEF Collegiate Institute

These intensive three-, four-, or five-day programs in direct marketing theory and practice are conducted for college juniors, seniors, or graduate students. Details can be found on the DMEF web site (www.the-dma.org/dmef), by contacting DMEF at 212/768-7277, extension 1817, or by contacting a business-related professor at the university.

Attending the Collegiate Institute can measurably speed up a career. Among the Institute's graduates are dozens of top-level agency and client-side personnel, including Heather Burgett of the Reader's Digest and Karl Dentino of Rosenfield/Dentino, both profiled in Chapter 11.

DMEF Summer Internship Program

Stimulating internships in mailing list maintenance, marketing research, account services, telemarketing, subscription fulfillment, copywriting, production, media, and other areas of direct marketing are available to recent graduates. These eight-to-ten-week direct marketing jobs offer a salary, on-the-job experience, and the opportunity to enrich your direct marketing knowledge through a series of afternoon seminars led by industry professionals.

Check the DMEF web site or your college career placement center for DMEF's National Directory of Summer Internships.

The application process varies by company, and final decisions remain with the individual companies.

College Days

Held in conjunction with the Direct Marketing Association's Annual and Net.Marketing conferences, College Days give students and professors the opportunity to attend one day of regular sessions, free of charge. Advanced registration is required.

When DMA Direct Marketing Days are held in New York, for example, the DMEF invites colleges and universities within a day's drive to be the DMEF's guest for the day's activities, lunch, and a special program on career opportunities in direct marketing. When the annual event is held in Chicago, schools in the surrounding area are contacted. Ask your professor to keep an eye out for the invitation.

Leonard J. Raymond Direct Marketing Collegiate "Echo" Competition

Cosponsored by the DMA Echo Awards Committee, the DMEF, and an annual corporate sponsor, the Collegiate ECHO competition gives students hands-on experience in actual direct marketing situations. Teams of four students are assigned a marketing problem and asked to solve it with direct or integrated marketing. The winning team receives all-expense-paid trips to the DMA's Annual Conference and Exhibition; second place entrants attend their local Direct Marketing Days event; and third place entrants are given direct marketing books and materials.

Student Membership in the DMA

Full-time students are eligible for one-year memberships. For $25 per year, students receive a membership card, discounts on

DMA conferences, and the following benefits: access to DMA's Direct Link abstracting service; *The DMA Insider,* a quarterly publication focusing on the latest trends, techniques, and issues; career information and resources; and choice of one DMA Council newsletter. Information and applications are available on the DMEF web site.

PROFESSIONAL ASSOCIATION EDUCATIONAL PROGRAMS

The Direct Marketing Association
1120 Avenue of the Americas
New York, NY 10036-6700
www.the-dma.org

The Direct Marketing Association is the professional association for direct marketers in the United States. It offers professional development seminars for direct marketers. These top-notch seminars, while expensive, offer superb coverage of the major areas of direct marketing. Each one is taught by recognized experts. Except for the Basic Institute, which is offered in different cities throughout the year, most courses are offered two to four times a year in Chicago and New York.

- **DMA Basic Institute.** A three-day immersion course that presents the fundamentals of successful direct marketing, from planning to fulfillment, and introduces the industry. Offered six times yearly in New York, Chicago, Atlanta, Washington DC, St. Louis, and other major cities.
- **Beyond the Basics.** An intensive blend of lecture, case study, and hands-on experience that teaches advanced strategies necessary to build a successful direct marketing business.
- **E-Commerce 101.** A one-day survey of the e-commerce landscape introduces today's cyber customers and explains

how to develop a long-term e-commerce strategy, develop effective on-line customer service, and market a web site.

- **E-Mail Marketing 101.** Explores e-mail marketing techniques and shows how to build on-line mailing lists, write e-mail messages, and integrate e-mail marketing into business and consumer marketing plans.

- **Managing Internet Marketing.** How to use the Internet for publicity, selling, customer service, support, training, advertising, fulfillment, lead generation and qualification, as well as how to build and run an Internet site.

- **Catalog Basics.** Offered twice a year, this course covers the essentials of catalog marketing, from up-front organization and matching merchandise and prices to a target audience, to converting prospects to customers and analyzing results.

- **Winning Direct Mail.** A two-day seminar on creating powerful, profitable direct mail packages.

- **Printing and Production: Buying and Planning for Direct Marketers.** A one-day seminar on the basics of production, including communicating with printers, negotiating prices, and producing a high-quality product economically.

- **Fulfillment and Customer Service Excellence.** Two one-day seminars on how to make fulfillment and customer service help increase sales, profits, and customers.

- **Profitable and Effective Use of the Telephone: Outbound and Inbound.** This three-day seminar offers a complete blueprint for using the telephone for outbound and inbound marketing and sales.

- **Frequency Marketing.** A two-day seminar on identifying best customers and building a frequency/loyalty program designed to build customer loyalty and grow profits.

- **Knowledge Discovery and Data Mining: Advanced Methods and Applications.** A two-day immersion in using response analysis to extract essential marketing information from a database and to prospect with geographic models.

- **Database Marketing.** A two-day seminar that introduces database techniques that can dramatically improve a company's profit picture. No technical knowledge is required.
- **Direct Marketing Math and Finance.** The basics of direct marketing math and finance are presented in a two-day seminar that demonstrates how to use direct marketing numbers, apply financial modeling techniques, and succeed in quantitative analysis.
- **Statistics and Modeling for Direct Marketers.** Two-day seminar on using statistical techniques, selecting and implementing the correct modeling method, and running sophisticated tests.
- **Modern Methods of Data Analysis and Response Modeling.** A one-day session on advanced statistics and how they can be integrated into predictive response models.
- **Insurance Direct Marketing.** A one-day seminar on targeting and selling insurance to customers and turning a one-policy customer into a long-term, multiproduct client.
- **The Laws Affecting Credit and Collection.** A one-day seminar that clarifies what can and cannot be done in extending credit and collecting debts.
- **The Law and Direct Marketing.** A one-day briefing on the laws, regulations, and legal issues that govern direct marketing business practices.
- **The DMA Certificate in Direct Marketing.** To promote across-the-board knowledge and practical expertise, the DMA awards a special certificate to candidates with a minimum of one year's experience in direct marketing who have earned ten seminar credits within thirty-six months.

The Canadian Marketing Association
1 Concorde Gate, Suite 607
Don Mills, Ontario M3C 3N6
Canada
www.the-cma.org

The CMA sponsors the following one-day courses, all taught by Canadian direct marketing professionals:

- Introduction to Direct Marketing
- Beyond the Basics of Direct Marketing
- Database Marketing
- Internet Marketing
- Data Mining

CHAPTER 11

GETTING STARTED

"Although almost every first job is difficult to get because of lack of experience, direct marketing has an advantage that most other industries do not," says the Direct Marketing Association. "It is testable, measurable, and accountable. And that can lead to rapid advancement." In other words, the trouble you take to find a challenging entry-level position can pay off in spades.

This chapter looks at the career paths of four direct and interactive marketing professionals and lays out a plan for finding and landing a great direct marketing job.

HOW THEY GOT THERE: FOUR CAREER PROFILES

Heather Burgett, Vice President and Publisher
Reader's Digest Home Video Products and Young Families

When Heather Burgett discovered direct marketing at the University of Cincinnati, she knew she had stumbled on a good thing. Enrollment in the Direct Marketing Educational Foundation's Collegiate Institute and a DMEF-sponsored internship at Doubleday Book Clubs led to her first job as a media analyst for Doubleday, where she identified prospective members using Doubleday's customer file and rented lists.

Two years as an Account Supervisor at Muldoon Direct broadened her knowledge of direct marketing. Under the tutelage of catalog consultant Katie Muldoon, Heather helped launch catalogs for General Mills and the John Deere Company. Start-ups were a fun challenge for Heather. "I enjoyed the big picture of catalog development and found it exciting to work with nontraditional businesses that recognized catalogs could retain customers, develop brand loyalty, and make a profit."

From Muldoon Direct, Heather moved to Reader's Digest, where she has steadily climbed up the organization. She began in circulation, where she prospected for millions of new customers a year. "The *Reader's Digest* subscription base then was over sixteen million," she explains. "But subscriptions expire constantly, so we had to bring in hundreds of thousands of new customers every month." Three years later she was traveling the world as Manager, International Magazine Circulation, recommending circulation strategies to *Reader's Digest* circulation managers in France, Switzerland, and other countries. "I was young and managers were often skeptical when they first met me. But my renewals and prospecting record spoke for itself. This business is all about results!"

With five years of circulation experience under her belt, Heather became Senior Product Manager for Home Video Products, where she developed mailing packages and sweepstakes offers for customers and prospects. "I supervised creative, advertising, list selection, everything but video production," she remembers. A year later, as Marketing Director, New Business Development, she launched programs in new marketing channels to grow the company's customer base. She supervised production of television commercials used to sell the Digest's core product mix via direct response broadcast, a new marketing and distribution channel for Reader's Digest. And most important, she reduced the time to market for new marketing campaigns in half, from test to roll-out.

"Time to market is essential to results," she explains. "The faster a campaign is up and rolling, the better."

Today, as Vice President and Publisher of Reader's Digest Home Video and Reader's Digest Young Families, Heather has line responsibility for two large businesses. "In direct marketing, the results are always measurable. Successes and failures can always be traced back to you," she says. "I like seeing the impact I've had on the businesses I've run."

For most of her ten years at Reader's Digest, Heather has been involved in starting up or growing new businesses. "New business development is my primary interest," she says. "I really enjoy applying direct marketing to new products, channels, and markets."

Her advice to newcomers? "Get hooked up with the DMEF. It's a terrific organization. Read all the trade journals, including general advertising publications like *Advertising Age.* Go to small businesses and organizations and volunteer your direct marketing services. That way you'll have some successes and failures under your belt before you ever start looking for a real job."

Jonathan Sackett, Director of Interactive Services, Townsend Agency

Jonathan Sackett didn't get into his field intentionally. "It came to me," he says. "Companies are desperate for people who understand interactive technology and can articulate it. I'm a marketing guy who understands the technology, not a technical person. That has opened doors for me."

Doors started opening when he joined Software Elements, a pioneer in web site development at a time when the Internet was primarily inhabited by scientists and programmers. "I found myself dealing with technical people with no relational skills, or people with strong relational skills and no technical grounding.

People could give me an idea but not execute it, or execute a program but not come up with ideas."

In response to the vacuum, Jonathan began combining his marketing education and his new technical skills to develop theoretical solutions to business problems. Each new assignment led to a new discovery. When he helped the company devise ways to use the Internet to update its database by designing compelling programs that encouraged customers to enter information about themselves, for example, he discovered that on-line data collection was many times more effective than traditional mail-in surveys.

Internet technology was maturing when Jonathan moved to Milwaukee interactive agency SpecterCom, where he helped design a virtual aquarium for Tetra Products. "What I had done before was nothing compared to this!" he notes. "Our site let people select fish that had preprogrammed behaviors and populate an aquarium so they could see what owning one would be like." Inspired by that experience, Jonathan began using the Internet for on-line research, targeted e-mail, customer service, and branding.

At Townsend Agency, which he joined in 1998, Jonathan supervises digital marketing campaigns that take advantage of the Internet, Intranet, Extranet, CD Roms, and CD cards (CD Roms that are the size and shape of a credit card). The results are exciting. "On-line programs offer infinite ways to tailor messages to specific customers. For GTE, which offers eleven different cellular calling programs, we created an on-line campaign that offers individual incentives to customers depending on their usage patterns. When customers visit the web site and use a password, the database retrieves information that tells us whether someone has used GTE Airfone three times or ten, and then makes a specific offer. If we used traditional direct mail, we'd have to offer fewer incentives to larger groups of people and would lose money."

Jonathan is looking forward to using cutting-edge technology to refine on-line direct marketing techniques. "It's the ultimate one-to-one marketing strategy," he concludes.

Karl Dentino, President, Rosenfield/Dentino Inc.

What's the best way to find a job in direct marketing? If you're Karl Dentino, you rely on...direct marketing!

After graduating with a degree in communications from New Jersey's Glassboro State College, Karl was awarded a scholarship to the Direct Marketing Educational Foundations' 1978 Collegiate Institute. Hooked by direct marketing at once, he decided to go into the field.

Dentino wondered how in the world he could get employers' attention in a difficult job market—especially since he had an undergraduate degree, not an M.B.A., and it wasn't from a well-known university. After reflecting on what he had learned from the Collegiate Institute, Karl decided to compose a one-page mailing to send to prospective employers.

The headline, "Here Are Five Profitable Reasons Why You Should Hire This Adman" appeared over a box listing the reasons:

1. Experience (his resume)
2. Advertising skills
3. Education
4. Leadership qualities
5. Self-motivation.

The rest of the mailing presented his advertising philosophy and invited the prospect to fill out the enclosed reply card or call for a free demonstration of "Karl's selling abilities."

Twenty-three letters later, he received eleven interviews, two job offers, and a Bronze DMA Echo Award for a job search program.

In his first job at The Direct Marketing Group, he mastered production and account services. At Benton & Bowles Direct, he gained package goods experience by helping to develop Procter & Gamble's first direct marketing venture. He began his four and one-half years at Wunderman Worldwide as account executive on Merrill Lynch, eventually becoming account supervisor on CBS

Columbia House (the record and video club), General Foods' Gevalia Coffee, and the U.S. Army.

In 1987, he was asked to start up the East Coast office of Rosenfield/Vinson Direct, an agency now known as Rosenfield/Dentino Inc. As president and partner, he directs all client-related account management activities, which involves developing new business and supervising account, creative, production, and administrative personnel. In 1989, he received the first U.S. Young Direct Marketer of the Year Scholarship, which enabled him to visit a number of leading direct marketing companies throughout the country and discuss direct response strategies and approaches with their top management.

Karl is a much-in-demand lecturer and teacher whose recent speeches at conferences held by the Direct Marketing Association, Bank Marketing Association, New Zealand Marketing Association, and others have been highly acclaimed. He also is noted for his work in educating students on behalf of the DMEF. In 1994 he was appointed Dean of their flagship educational program, the Direct Marketing Collegiate Institute, and he has served on the DMEF board of trustees since 1997. His book, *Business Reply: How to Use Direct Marketing Techniques to Get the Job You Want,* was published in 1995.

His advice to people trying to break into direct marketing is to approach the job hunt the same way a marketing manager approaches a direct marketing program. "The more you view the process as 'generating leads and selling' instead of 'resumes and interviewing,' the more successful you'll be."

Phil Herring: President, Herring/Newman, Inc.

As a bass trombone player for the Stan Kenton band, which he joined when he was eighteen, Phil Herring packed 320 one-nighters into fifty weeks a year on the road. But after two years of constant travel, he was ready for a rest—so he founded a music publishing company that eventually merged with Stan Kenton's. During his six years in publishing, he began to use direct marketing techniques, which he continued to rely on during a two-year stint in artist management and concert promotion.

At twenty-nine, Phil decided he'd had enough of the music business. But what could he do instead? On reflection, he realized that his direct marketing experience could serve him well in a career in advertising. "Getting out of the music business and into something else was the most difficult juncture of my career," Phil confesses. "But I managed to convince Walt Disney Telecommunications that my publishing background and direct marketing experience could serve them well."

At Disney, he helped launch Disney Home Video and the Disney Channel. Eventually, he decided to relocate to Seattle, where he joined Seafirst Bank as a direct marketer.

"It was at Seafirst that I realized that I had a career going in direct marketing—and that I liked it. Unfortunately, six months after I started, I was laid off." Soon after, he started Seattle's first direct marketing agency. As he tells it, he christened the agency Northwest Communications Group because "back then, no one knew if a direct marketer could actually make a living in Seattle. The name was chosen to keep one's options open."

Today, his agency, Herring/Newman, is a highly regarded source of sophisticated, motivating, and effective work. It employs fifty people, has billings of $35 million, and has won a host of coveted awards from Gold Echos and a Gold Mailbox (awarded for "the world's most innovative use of direct mail") to John Caples Awards and, most recently, an Honor Award from the American Institute of Architects (AIA) for its concrete, raw steel, and plywood offices.

"When I announced my plans to move to Seattle, an illustrator I represented shook his head and said, 'You know, there are people who want to be the best and the brightest in an industry, and they go to New York or Los Angeles. Then there are people like you, who move to Seattle.'

"The funny thing is that anything I've done of significance has been in Seattle. I've had so many people tell me that it would have been much harder to do the kind of work I do in Los Angeles, where pressures to conform are greater. But being in a secondary market has its advantages. If you look around, you'll see that in direct marketing and advertising, the best creative shops are not in the biggest cities."

On launching a career in direct marketing, he comments, "From an employer's point of view, the people I love to hire are just starting out. They very clearly have a burning desire to be in direct marketing. They know the agencies, and they know the advertising they like. To them, direct marketing is almost a hobby. These people stand out from the rest, who just walk in looking for a job and think advertising might be fun."

HOW YOU CAN GET IN

The Direct Marketing Educational Foundation urges prospective direct marketers to follow a five-point plan for mastering the basics of direct marketing and becoming an attractive prospective employee. The five points are as follows:

1. Take a basic direct marketing course through a college, university, or professional association.
2. Serve an internship with a direct marketing–related company.
3. Enter student marketing competitions such as the Collegiate Echo competition.
4. Read pertinent books and periodicals.
5. Collect a "swipe" file of effective direct marketing promotions.

When it's time to look for work, there are two more points to pursue:

1. Research individual companies using the Direct Marketing Marketplace and the agency "red book."
2. Join a local direct marketing club to network with members and access their job referral services.

Courses, internships, and student competitions are discussed in Chapter 10. Local direct marketing clubs are listed in Appendix A; references are cited in Appendix C.

Learn from the Masters

"Those who aspire to new heights of direct marketing creativity should first climb onto the shoulders of the great practitioners of the past and present," encourages Susan K. Jones in her book, *Creative Strategy in Direct Marketing*. It's just one of dozens of excellent manuals that cover every aspect of direct marketing, from constructing appealing offers and crafting copy that sells to using databases and selecting lists.

A few of the great books are listed in Appendix C. Most are available through bookstores or libraries or may be ordered directly from the Direct Marketing Association.

Start a Swipe File

If you're interested in a career in direct marketing, start a swipe file right now.

A swipe file is your personal collection of direct mail pieces, self-mailers, catalogs, and space ads that intrigue you. If you're a mail-order consumer, most of these pieces will be sent to you for free. All you'll have to do is stop and examine each one, looking for packages you think are pulling well or beating control.

Collect a variety from all segments of the market—consumer electronics, sporting goods, food, clothing, office supplies, books and videos, and collectibles. Analyze them, looking for what works: a real grabber of a headline, an unbeatable synthesis of copy and words, an offer that can't be turned down. As you collect these pieces, you'll be refining your taste in direct marketing.

The greatest swipe file around belongs to the Direct Marketing Association. Three years' worth of winners of the prestigious Echo Awards are on file in the DMA's Information Central, indexed by agency, advertiser, and product category. Employees of DMA member companies can borrow and study up to six portfolios of winning campaigns.

Each portfolio contains the actual creative package, along with information on the rationale behind the strategy and execution, the media used, and the response earned by the campaign—valuable background for any direct marketer interested in learning from the successes of others.

Creatives: Make a Portfolio

If you're aspiring to a career as a copywriter or art director, it's imperative to start a portfolio. Your prospective employers will want to see firsthand how you approach and solve marketing problems.

Your portfolio should include samples of your best work, including direct mail space ads, packages, or storyboards that do the following:

- illustrate a variety of products
- come from several campaigns
- employ a number of different creative approaches and creative and media executions
- list media choices and explain why they were chosen

A good resource for portfolio compilers is *The Advertising Portfolio* by Ann Marie Barry.

Use the DMA Job Bank

For an up-to-date sense of what's available, check the DMA Job Bank. Access the list at www.the-dma.org by clicking on the "Job Bank" button, and then clicking on "job opportunities." The Bank lists available positions in direct and interactive marketing companies. Although many of the jobs require experience, from time to time entry-level openings are included.

Network, Network, Network

Executive search specialist Nancy Wright-Nelson believes that a job search is an appropriate time to shake the trees for contacts who can help you. Ask friends, parents, neighbors, even the mail carrier if they know people in direct marketing you can talk to. When you run out of personal connections, turn to your local direct marketing club.

Most clubs and professional associations offer formal or informal job networks that publicize openings and people who are seeking work. In addition, almost every club meeting is a networking event of some kind. Before, during, and after the program, club members have plenty of opportunities to meet informally and swap business cards, discuss business trends, and introduce their businesses.

Anyone who is serious about a career in direct marketing should affiliate with the closest club as soon as possible and make it the cornerstone of networking efforts.

WHAT EMPLOYERS ARE LOOKING FOR

Every position has its own list of duties and responsibilities, and every company has its own culture. So even though there are prerequisites for entering direct marketing, the criteria behind a decision to hire vary from company to company.

Each of the direct marketing professionals who contributed materials to this book has strong feelings about the qualities they are seeking in new employees, as well as how prospective employees should approach them. Their observations follow.

Know Your Stuff

To Rich Vergara of The Kleid Company, education in direct marketing is a critical distinguishing factor. "If I were looking at ten recent business school graduates and one of them had bothered to take a few direct marketing courses, that would be the one I would hire. With so many colleges and universities offering direct marketing courses, and so many seminars available from professional associations, people interested in direct marketing ought to show a little initiative and complete at least one course before looking for a job."

A catalog executive agrees. "Most young people I talk to haven't got the slightest idea what direct marketing is. I'm shocked to meet applicants who not only don't know a thing about the field, but haven't taken time to seek out its basic tenets. I recommend that anyone seeking a job in a nontraditional selling channel like direct marketing bone up on it first. An applicant has to bring a little something to the party to avoid exasperating a potential employer."

Graduate education is especially helpful. Executive recruiter Nancy Wright-Nelson believes that a master's degree will add 10 to 15 percent to a salary. A master's in direct marketing, now available at a handful of institutions, also commands a higher salary, but its value can be even greater in the long run—over the course of a career.

Show That You Can Juggle Balls

The Bradford Exchange looks for signs that a prospective employee can cope with many responsibilities simultaneously.

"We look for enthusiastic people who can juggle many activities at once," says one of its employment managers. "Extracurricular activities are important. Someone who demonstrates that they can carry a full load of classes and still find time for clubs and interest groups will catch our eye. Marketing degrees are important, too, and internships of any kind will make a difference."

Master Technology and Develop a Strong Marketing Sense

Companies want people who understand technology and know how to use it. If you're pursuing a technical degree, look for courses in web application programming. Cross over to the marketing department, and enroll in a database marketing course. "You'll learn how to create and analyze a database, both invaluable skills in interactive business," says Jonathan Sackett, Director of Interactive Services for Townsend Agency. "You need to be able to understand how to draw information from the database to develop customer profiles and analyze purchase patterns and response."

Prospective copywriters and art directors also need to be adept at computers. At many catalog companies, copywriters are responsible for producing finished pages on page-layout software using templates provided by designers. Interactive art directors must understand how to marry technical programs with great design.

But don't let the dazzling opportunities of the Internet obscure the importance of marketing strategy. Companies also want people who know how to build a brand and form an overall marketing strategy that encompasses a variety of media—people who can integrate on-line selling into an overall marketing strategy.

And don't drop out of school. Even though the newspapers are filled with stories of eighteen-year-olds making their fortunes in Internet businesses, a formal education still means a lot. "It takes broad-based knowledge to develop the kind of marketing solutions we provide," says Jonathan Sackett.

Polish Your Ability to Cope with Near-Constant Change

Demonstrate that you're at home with the on-line, "24/7 mind-set" and can keep up with the incredible rate of change that characterizes our times. Your ability to roll with the punches is a great asset in a world in which the Internet lets orders be placed and shipped immediately, strategies are developed in the blink of an eye, and a marketing campaign that once took a leisurely twelve months to develop is conceived and executed in sixty exhausting days.

"The pace of change can drive us to make decisions that aren't necessarily thought out," says Tim Claffey, Executive Vice President, Managing Director, Leo Burnett NorthStar. "People are so afraid of being left behind that they react to the pace of change in ways that may not be good for business."

Employers like NorthStar want people who are comfortable with constant change rather than intimidated by it. "We need smart, energetic people who can adapt quickly," says Claffey, who has noticed that new college graduates seem to be used to the pace of change. Look for ways to demonstrate that you can roll with the punches and use good judgment about when change is—and isn't—necessary.

Persist, Creatively

To Patrice Lyon, Ogilvy & Mather Direct's Senior Vice President, Network Development, persistence counts. "Direct marketing is establishing and maintaining a dialogue in a relationship. The people we hire understand that. They manage the job search process the same way they manage a direct marketing campaign—as more than just a short-term enterprise.

"People assume that a campaign to join an agency like OMD ends when the company turns them down. They think, 'I didn't get the job, it's over with.' But that's just not true. People who keep in touch with us in an imaginative way—even if they don't get a positive response from us right off the bat—can eventually succeed.

"By 'keeping in touch' I don't mean just calling me to see what's happening. I mean reminding me that you're there in an imaginative, innovative way—like Karl Dentino did in his job campaign."

A recent OMD hire came to Ms. Lyon's attention because she knew an OMD copywriter. As part of her campaign to land a job at OMD, she sent Ms. Lyon notes and objects celebrating offbeat holidays: a good luck token on a Friday the 13th, a want ad painted on an egg for Easter. She used a succession of different ideas and formats in her campaign to enter OMD—and she succeeded.

"I'm keeping track of three or four people right now. Each of them is doing something that keeps them in mind as often as possible. Out of all the people trying to get hired at Ogilvy right now, they're probably the only ones who have made that difference."

Persistence is a valuable quality to nurture throughout a direct marketing career. Just ask Ross Longendyke, who was laid off from three jobs in a row. "I had been in the wrong place at the wrong time for three straight years, but I didn't get discouraged," he says. "I knew this was a healthy, growing industry that interested me. I remained optimistic that everything would work out, remembering that hard work and persistence are what get anybody ahead."

JUMP-START YOUR CAREER: WIN THE YOUNG DIRECT MARKETER OF THE YEAR SCHOLARSHIP

This exciting program offers young direct marketing professionals a chance to earn considerable recognition and one-on-one meetings in the executive suites of the United States' leading direct marketing companies.

Sponsored by Kobs and Draft Advertising and administered by the Direct Marketing Association's International Council, the scholarship is open to professionals under thirty. Candidates, each one nominated and seconded by superiors, must have been employed in direct marketing for at least three years to be eligible.

A panel of experts reviews all applications, selects three finalists for personal interviews, and then chooses a winner whose achievements and initiative are outstanding. The winner receives a two-week, all-expense-paid tour of the top direct marketing companies around the country, discussing strategies and approaches with their top executives. The tour culminates in the city where the DMA's conference is held.

Nominees for the award come from all areas of direct marketing, as do the judges. Winners have come from direct marketing agencies, telemarketing companies, and catalog companies.

For more information, contact the DMA's International Council or Kobs & Draft Advertising.

REMEMBER, THE FUTURE IS BRIGHT

Direct and interactive marketing is a dynamic field whose prospects grow brighter each day. New applications for direct marketing, interactive, and database techniques as well as new positions for the people who practice them are constantly being created.

As Karl Dentino notes, "In spite of the fact that direct marketing has been around for more than a century, we're just beginning to learn how to apply it to nontraditional categories like package goods and consumer products. The future for direct marketing is very bright indeed."

DIRECT MARKETING CLUBS AND ASSOCIATIONS

PROFESSIONAL ASSOCIATIONS

Direct Marketing Association, Inc.
1120 Avenue of the Americas
New York, NY 10036-6700
(212) 768-7277
www.the-dma.org

The leading professional association in the industry, the Direct Marketing Association represents direct marketers in legislative and government affairs, tracks trends, makes current statistics on direct marketing available through its library, and provides professional education to members and nonmembers alike.

Canadian Marketing Association
One Concord Gate, Suite 607
Toronto, Ontario
Canada M3C 3N6
(416) 391-2362
www.the-cma.org

The CMA serves as an industry advocate on legislative and public issues, as a self-regulatory body, and as a major source of continuing education for Canadian direct marketing professionals. Its special interest councils focus on business-to-business marketing, catalogs, financial services, fund-raising, insurance, lettershops, the list industry, the publishing industry, and telemarketing.

Women in Direct Marketing International

Through its chapters in Chicago, New York, and Washington DC, WDMI provides networking opportunities, business contacts, and a forum for industry practitioners. Entry-level direct marketers are encouraged to join and become active. To contact current leadership, call the DMA's Clubs and Associations Network.

REGIONAL DIRECT MARKETING CLUBS

Regional direct marketing clubs offer stimulating monthly meetings where a variety of direct marketing topics are discussed. Most publish newsletters, offer a job search network to members seeking employment, and conduct annual or semiannual direct marketing fairs where industry members gather for seminars, networking, and trade exhibits. Some sponsor educational programs; others sponsor them in conjunction with a local college or university.

Regional direct marketing clubs offer newcomers a chance to get to know local industry personnel, enhance their direct marketing knowledge, and gain visibility through club activities, committees, and awards programs.

In the list that follows, addresses and telephone numbers are provided for clubs with full-time executive staff and office space. Other clubs and chapters are run by volunteer leaders who turn over annually. To contact them, ask the DMA's Clubs and Associations Network for the name of the current president.

Arizona
Phoenix Direct Marketing Club

California
Direct Marketing Club of Southern California
Northern California Direct Marketing Club
Direct Marketing Association of Orange County

Colorado
Rocky Mountain Direct Marketing Association

Connecticut
Direct Marketing Association of Western Connecticut
New England Mail Order Association

District of Columbia
Direct Marketing Association of Washington
Women in Direct Marketing International

Florida
Florida Direct Marketing Association
   Central Florida Chapter (Orlando area)
   Gold Coast Chapter (Miami–Fort Lauderdale area)
   Suncoast Chapter (Tampa–St. Petersburg–Sarasota area)

Georgia
Direct Marketing Association of Atlanta

Hawaii
Direct Response Advertising & Marketing Association of Hawaii

Illinois
Chicago Association of Direct Marketing
Women in Direct Marketing International

Indiana

Direct Marketing Association of Indianapolis

Kentucky

Louisville Direct Marketing Association

Maryland

Maryland Direct Marketing Association

Massachusetts

New England Direct Marketing Association

Michigan

Direct Marketing Association of Detroit

Minnesota

Midwest Direct Marketing Association

Missouri

Direct Marketing Association of St. Louis

Kansas City Direct Marketing Association

Nebraska

Mid-America Direct Marketing Association

New York

Direct Marketing Club of New York

Hudson Valley Direct Marketing Club

Long Island Direct Marketing Club

Upstate New York Direct Marketing Association

Women in Direct Marketing International

Ohio

Cincinnati Direct Marketing Club

Dayton Direct Marketing Club

Mid-Ohio Direct Marketing Association

Oregon
Oregon Direct Marketing Association

Pennsylvania
Philadelphia Direct Marketing Association

Texas
Dallas/Ft. Worth Direct Marketing Association
Houston Direct Marketing Association

Vermont/New Hampshire
Vermont/New Hampshire Direct Marketing Group

Washington
Seattle Direct Marketing Association
Spokane Direct Mail Marketing Association

Wisconsin
Wisconsin Direct Marketing Club

TOP-RANKING DIRECT MARKETING AGENCIES

According to the Direct Marketing Association's Research Department, these twenty-four agencies led the field of direct marketing, interactive, and database agencies that reported their 1998 billings to the DMA.

Agencies	Total 1998 Billings (in millions)	U.S. Billings (in millions)	International Billings (in millions)
1. Brann Worldwide	$2,712.8	$1,900.2	$812.6
2. Rapp Collins Worldwide	1,837.0	861.9	975.1
3. Carlson Marketing Group	864.5	593.3	271.2
4. Targetbase Marketing	376.6	354.5	22.1
5. Customer Development Corp.	241.1	241.1	NA
6. Grizzard Communications Group	199.3	194.0	5.3
7. Brierley & Partners	194.9	190.5	4.4
8. Hill Holliday	114.7	114.7	NA

Agencies	Total 1998 Billings (in millions)	U.S. Billings (in millions)	International Billings (in millions)
9. Cohn & Wells Inc.	114.6	114.6	NA
10. CPS Direct, Inc.	99.4	99.4	NA
11. Colleagues Direct Marketing Ltd. (UK)	94.7	NA	94.7
12. RTCdirect	87.5	87.5	NA
13. Creative Marketing International, a Division of Aspen Marketing Group	85.7	85.7	NA
14. Beyond DDB	70.8	70.8	NA
15 TargetCom, Inc.	65.7	65.7	NA
16. Lieber, Levett, Koenig, Farese, Babcock, Inc.	53.2	53.2	NA
17. Martin Direct	48.2	48.2	NA
18. M2Direct	28.2	28.2	NA
19. Bullseye Database Marketing Inc.	19.2	19.2	NA
20. Clienting Group (Argentina)	15.0	NA	15.0
21. Archer/Malmo Direct	14.8	14.8	NA
22. Manus Direct	13.1	13.1	NA
23. DiPaola & Asociados S.A. (Argentina)	6.5	NA	6.5
24. Rumba Direct	3.6	3.6	NA

RECOMMENDED READING

BOOKS

Godin, Seth. *Permission Marketing.* New York: Simon & Schuster, 1999.

Jackson, Rob and Wang, Paul. *Strategic Database Marketing.* Chicago: NTC/Contemporary Publishing, 1994.

Jones, Susan K. *Creative Strategy in Direct Marketing,* second edition. Chicago: NTC/Contemporary Publishing, 1998.

Kobs, Jim. *Profitable Direct Marketing.* Chicago: NTC/Contemporary Publishing, 1992.

Schmid, Jack. *Starting and Growing a Profitable Catalog.* Chicago: NTC/Contemporary Publishing, 2000.

Schultz, Don E. *Integrated Marketing Methods: Putting It Together and Making It Work.* Chicago: NTC/Contemporary Publishing, 1993.

Stone, Bob. *Successful Direct Marketing Methods,* sixth edition. Chicago: NTC/Contemporary Publishing, 1997.

Throckmorton, Joan. *Winning Direct Response Advertising: From Print through Interactive Media.* Chicago: NTC/Contemporary Publishing, 1997.

Vernon, Lillian. *An Eye for Winners: How I Built One of America's Greatest Direct-Mail Businesses.* New York: HarperCollins, 1997.

PERIODICALS

Advertising Age
Crain Communications
740 North Rush Street
Chicago, IL 60611

American Demographics
P.O. Box 68
Ithaca, NY 14851-0068

Canadian Direct Marketing News
1200 Markham Road #301
Scarborough, Ontario M1H 3C3
Canada

Catalog Age
P.O. Box 4949
Stamford, CT 06907-0949

Direct
470 Park Avenue South, 7th Floor North
New York, NY 10016-6819

Direct Marketing Magazine
Hoke Communications
224 Seventh Street
Garden City, NY 11530

DM News
100 Avenue of the Americas, 6th floor
New York, NY 10013-1689

The Friday Report
Hoke Communications
224 Seventh Street
Garden City, NY 11530

Target Marketing
401 North Broad Street
Philadelphia, PA 19108-1087